T0199085

What Your Daddy Never Told You and Your Mother Never Knew

Spiritual Techniques to Recover All

Romonica Jones

WESTBOW
PRESS®
A DIVISION OF THOMAS NELSON
& ZONDERVAN

WestBow Press books may be ordered through
booksellers or by contacting:

WestBow Press
A Division of Thomas Nelson & Zondervan
1663 Liberty Drive
Bloomington, IN 47403
www.westbowpress.com
1 (866) 928-1240

ISBN: 978-1-9736-6077-4 (sc)
ISBN: 978-1-9736-6078-1 (hc)
ISBN: 978-1-9736-6076-7 (e)

Library of Congress Control Number: 2019904646

Print information available on the last page.

WestBow Press rev. date: 07/08/2019

Preface

What your mother did not know and what your father never told you is that more than anything, you are beautiful, loved, worthy, valuable, unique, distinctive, capable, able, strong, loving, kind, caring, giving, gifted, talented, gorgeous, intelligent, whole, stable, reliable, consistent, nurturing, hardworking, meaningful, courageous, a visionary, classy, respectful, evolutionary, ever evolving, ever growing, ever loving, ever learning, not easily broken, a survivor, a conqueror, fearfully and wonderfully made, exquisite, and delicate. You have the true essence of a queen or king, and you are necessary!

chapter 1

The Power and Purpose
of a Man or Woman

Any business owner, author, mother, or music or movie producer knows the true difficulties of producing a quality product, child, or service. It takes power to produce! I have quite often, like many, found myself in the birthing position. During such a time, I have experienced what felt like spiritual morning sickness, disconnected myself from toxic lifelong friendships that spoke against what I was birthing, and at one point found myself night after night sleeping on the floor on my prayer mat as that was the only comfortable position! Producing forced me to forsake comfortable beds and couches to sleep on a thin prayer mat. Being spiritually pregnant forced me to remain active in the spiritual realm as faith was my spiritual baby's life supply.

Many mothers have found themselves in the same position—and possibly even more intense. As their bodies stretch, they forsake draining relationships and environments for the betterment of the quality seed they carry. Morning sickness leads them to watch

1

their appetites. My spiritual appetite during that time drastically increased. Sometimes you realize that whatever you eat, as is common with morning sickness, just won't stay down! Mothers forsake their own comfort for their offspring, such as leaving jobs that will not allow them proper maternity leave, staying in difficult relationships to give their children a home or a two-parent lifestyle, facing fears of going back to school, and ending negative soul ties.

TV show and music producers awakening in the middle of the night write words that just won't come to mind during the lunch hour. With scriptwriters visiting the set late at night to truly capture the vision of the night scene you are producing, you often find yourself in a night season of your own life when you are spiritually pregnant! As a producer, you may hide pieces of yourself in each character and relive yet rewrite your own story through the lives of the on-screen characters. You're just as pregnant as the mother who's in the birthing position and screaming at her nurse or husband on set. The strokes of the politicians' pens change the course of life for millions—even whole nations. Being pregnant with or producing new laws, policies, amendments, and statutes (changing the face of health care, school systems, court rulings, and marriage law), deciding whether to go to war with countries or make peace—my goodness! That is true power! This goes back to my original statement that it takes power to produce, even more because what you are producing holds limitless potential! What you produce places focus on the power and purpose of a man and woman.

Women, you are powerful because you were created to do a hard thing; you were born to produce. Many women compete with one another because they have not determined that there is no competition, that no two people will produce the same thing. You are divinely unique, and your creation was and is truly necessary. What you carry—natural or spiritual—could never come forth without you. You are valuable!

chapter 2

Leah's Story

And he went in also unto Rachel, and he loved also Rachel more than Leah, and served with him yet seven other years. And when the Lord saw that Leah was hated, he opened her womb: but Rachel was barren.

—Genesis 29:30–31

When Leah was hated by her husband, God opened her womb so she might produce. The question is this: since the heart is in the King's hand, why didn't God make Jacob love Leah? God opened her womb because, in doing so, he increased her value. Bill Gates is valuable not just because of who he is but also because of what he has produced. Also, God was reminding Leah that she had been created to reproduce, as *wom(b)* is in the word *woman*, meaning a man with a womb. He was redirecting her to know that her purpose was in reproducing. That was the divine reason why she was created. She was loved by a man, family, children, coworkers, and an audience of one or many, but that was a lagniappe, because her purpose was not in who loved her but in her ability to produce! When the Lord saw that she was hated, he redirected her, opening her womb to hint to his daughter of her divine purpose. In essence, he was saying that her value was not in the love of a man but in her ability to do what he had created her to do, which was to produce.

What wound, hurt, pain, rejection, grief, or bitterness is consuming your time and thoughts? What in life is paralyzing your ability to produce what God created you to produce? Just like it was for Leah, what he has in store for you will automatically increase your value. Leah, overall, was more valuable than Rachel. Rachel was loved, but she envied Leah because although she was loved, her purpose was unfilled during the time she remained barren, unable to produce.

Additionally, where there is power, there also may be dread, intimidation, anxiety, and much fear. A former US president reported that one of his main concerns about an enemy of the United States was that they had weapons of mass destruction, which permitted the government to take the necessary steps to disarm that nation. How would that have been different if, instead of having weapons of mass destruction, they had had weapons of mass toothbrushes? Yes, that would have changed the whole dynamic in how the president handled such a nation. *Weapons of mass destruction* is a term that is a lot different from *weapons of mass toothbrushes* in that weapons of destruction have the power to destroy.

Seeing that women's power is in their ability to produce, many men have seen the woman they were created to protect, cover, and love as Christ loves the church as a threat (Ephesians 5:25). That fear, which is birthed out of vulnerability, has left many men feeling inferior, feeling intimidated, being controlling, and being abusive (physically and emotionally) as a way to even the score. As opposed to building the women up by encouraging them to produce, men have rejected them. These men have reminded the women of their limited societal role, degrading them by attempting to make them valuable only according to how sexually attractive they are and how they can be used by men. If men were to understand that they can be esteemed just as much for their ability to aid a woman in producing, they would get their value from helping a woman as opposed to hurting her.

Such industries that degrade the value of women have mastered this technique to meet the need of men and to fulfill the purpose of catering to men's perversion, often at the cost of the woman's full destiny, potential, or real identity. The perversion of the fantasy to see women's private body parts includes having women undress for men without the men hinting at marrying them, let alone following through and actually doing so. If society can get women to dress in tight shorts, low-cut blouses, and see-through clothing in public, then the women will become indoctrinated in a culture that makes it that much easier for men to undress women in private, thereby allowing men to easily sleep with women they do not respect and have no desire to marry. This fulfills the perverted fantasies of the men, who then discard the women who have served their purpose.

Out of this lust, nations of illegitimate kids have been born. Like Leah, the rejected women who buy into this scheme are looking for love, but if they would turn their focus to God and producing, then the man whom God assigned to come into their lives would find the value of what they are producing as opposed to devaluing their naked bodies. *Women, beloved, where is your value?* Men, the foregoing question does not exclude you. Why is your value in degrading women, as opposed to uplifting and investing in yourself? As the head of the family, your goal should be to advance your family and not oppress them, as in doing so you suffer as well. You, woman, were created to produce and to be a helpmate to your husband, not to be with a man who doesn't think enough of you to commit his hand in marriage to you. Men, likewise, never let a woman use you for money out of your need to be loved, because then you will have a prostitute and not a potential life mate!

To the women who allow themselves to be intimate with uncommitted men, how has this advanced you, fed your purpose, filled empty voids, or made you feel worthy, loved, or valued? How has sleeping with a man without commitment produced anything but regret and insecurities in you? How has it advanced your God-given purpose, beloved? Do you consider what the heavenly Father will say to you when you enter heaven? Will he say, "Servant, well done"? Lust may be socially acceptable, and it may be generationally widespread in your family, but have you ever asked yourself how it has helped you outside the moment? Are you now closer to a commitment? Does the man you are with value you more or less, beloved? Ask yourself, "How is this really working for me?"

To the men who have found themselves the protagonists of such work, be advised that the spirit you feed is the one that will lead. If you feed lust, then when your God-sent wife comes along, you will not be able to value her, and it may be more difficult for you to be sexually satisfied by her if your appetite remains extreme. Once you have had many women through feeding the spirit of lust, the door is open for you to try other sexual extremes. Lust can lead to perversion, STDs, secret shameful fantasies, AIDS, living a double life, homosexuality, child support payments, emotional turmoil, soul ties, a lack of peace, and distractions that disable your own ability to produce. Remember, the spirit you feed is the one that will lead. Are you being led by a perverted, demonic force? If so, know that the end of such a path is often destruction. "There is a way which seems right unto a man, but the end thereof are the ways of death" (Proverbs 14:12). God ordained marriage to fulfill your sexual desires.

I mentioned earlier that the fear and intimidation that men who are not aware of their own value may feel toward women is born out of men's vulnerability. "What vulnerability?" you may ask. The vulnerability that is necessary to open their hearts and lives and place them in the hand of a woman breeds vulnerability in and of itself.

> The second level of vulnerability is this: yes, it may be a man's world, but not a soul would be living, breathing, walking, or talking in it without the womb of a producing woman or a girl.

Men's vulnerability is also birthed out of feeling unneeded by a powerful, producing, self-sustaining woman, which breeds fear of abandonment. So, beloved woman, I ask you again why you are producing children. Why are you engaging in the act that brings forth children without this man committing his hand to you in marriage? Men, why aren't you the type of man who encourages a high level of self-esteem in your mate? Women, if the man you are with has not embraced or married you, which is a form of rejection, do you not know that what is produced from the union will quite likely be rejected as well?

The child of Rachel, the wife whom Jacob loved, was a child he loved and favored. Now Israel loved Joseph more than all Jacob's children because he was the son born in Jacob's old age. And Jacob made Joseph a coat of many colors. When a man loves, honors, respects, marries, and commits to you, you won't have to beg him to love the seed that was birthed out of your union with him. But when your union produces a child out of a lustful or demonically driven, sexually perverted experience, that seed—being the child—is often rejected as well. To wit, Leah's children hated Joseph because not only was their mother hated but also, because none of them were Jacob's favorite son, they felt hated as well. Dear mother, is that the foundation or springboard of rejection from which you want to produce your beloved children? If not, then let's break the cycle. Look for true committed love within yourself, which will attract that same type of love to you and then bring forth loved and embraced children out of a God-given and loving union. It was never God's will or intention for the love that you so willingly give and search for in others to be used against you or bring harm—whether mental, physical, spiritual, or emotional—to you. If this is what you are experiencing, then what type of environment have you provided for your children? Is it one in which they can excel and thrive? Have you fallen into this snare or open door by way of your own childhood rejection? Or maybe you have allowed yourself to be devalued and seen as worthless because you are searching for love. Trust me, I have been there, and I completely understand! The key here is to "love your neighbor as you love yourself." The way to do this is, first, by realizing that perverted lust is not love—nor does it feel like such. Second, how can you identify true love in others if you have not found it or been able to identify it within *yourself*, beloved? God is hinting to you that the degree to which you love yourself defines your ability to love your neighbor. But if you don't love and embrace yourself, how can you have the ability to know if your relationship is one that is truly built on love? We know that God so loved the world that he gave his only begotten Son. Therefore, we are armed with knowing that love is not self-seeking or self-serving but is founded on giving and not taking! What does your picture of someone loving you look like? Does it look like you protecting yourself from being in relationships with people who take and do not give back? Does it look like you investing in your own future, catering to yourself, going out to eat and to a movie by yourself, pampering yourself, treating yourself, building a savings account for a rainy day, educating yourself, and preparing yourself for the major promises of God?

An older coworker once asked me, "What do you want out of life?" I, being younger at the time, told her that I wanted a house, a car, a business, an overall nice lifestyle, to go on vacations, and to have a hefty savings. She looked into my young eyes and said, with the regretful eyes of a woman who wished someone would have asked her that very question at the age I was at the time, "Romonica, everything you just named—you are going to have to get those things for yourself." At that moment I stopped investing my entire future in temporarily assigned people and began to invest in myself. I purchased my first property at twenty years of age because I enjoy real estate; I opened up my first for-profit company at twenty-six years of age (Eclectic Counseling Services, now with two locations); I opened up my first nonprofit at twenty-seven years of age (Live Blessed Global Ministries); I graduated with a master's degree at twenty-five years of age; and shortly thereafter, I paid off my Mercedes-Benz. I found my value in producing. But whether I had accomplished any of the foregoing or not, I am still just as equally loved. In any event, I have found that faith without works is dead, and because I loved myself enough to acquire all the things I've named that I knew would make me happy, I went to work to ensure that I had those things regardless of who stayed or left (James 2:14).

Let's reevaluate. Beloved, you say you love yourself, but how are you really loving you? What is your evidence?

chapter 3

Hannah's Story

But to Hannah he would give a double
portion, because he loved Hannah, but the
Lord had given her no children. Hannah's
rival provoked her bitterly, to irritate and
embarrass her, because the Lord had left
her childless. So it happened year after
year, whenever she went up to the house of
the Lord, Peninnah provoked her; so she
wept and would not eat. Then Elkanah her
husband said to her, "Hannah, why do you
cry and why do you not eat? Why are you so
sad and discontent? Am I not better to you
than ten sons?"

—1 Samuel 1:5–8 (AB)

Hannah had love from her husband, but like Rachel,
she wrestled to produce. This baffled Hannah's
husband, who couldn't understand why she was grieved.
He asked her whether his show of love toward her wasn't

better than ten sons. Hannah continued to seek God to produce. In essence, Hannah had mastered how to discern the difference between her role as a beloved wife and her divine purpose to produce. Her husband's love was a means by which she was able to produce, by way of giving birth through their union, yet she did not confuse her means to produce (her husband) with the necessity and the missing value of her actual producing (a child).

chapter 4

Restoration

R epent and forgive yourself. Let's ask the question of how your unfaithful source of love has treated you. Does that reflect just how you have treated God? Commit and be faithful to the principles of God, and then watch God himself work out all things for you!

As if I had been alive at the time it was popular, I can vividly hear the lyrics of the song "Sexual Revolution." I can't help but notice that at the root of the word *revolution* is the word *revolt*. The song was written in revolt against the traditional practice of waiting until marriage to have sex, and of being the husband of one wife or the wife of one husband, two concepts that went completely out the window at the hands of an obviously perverted spirit that thought it a good idea for people to sleep with several different mates and not marry any of them—or to marry one of them yet sleep around. This has led us right up to the current era with numerous perversions, including same-sex relations, bestiality, child pornography, and sex slavery. Perversion crept in one door and of course didn't stop there. The single mother praying for a husband who will serve as a role model to her son sits in the audience as she watches two men marry each another. In her conscious thoughts, she reasons that one cannot control the free will of another. I still wonder if such commonality instills hope in that single, hopeful, faith-filled, praying woman. How we point the finger at one sin and not another. We point the finger at homosexuality but somehow leave out adultery, fornication, which has the ability to produce single parents bearing, in many cases, illegitimate children. Yes, my mother was a single parent, so I am speaking of single parenting as a whole. If I were to ask any single mother if she would like to have a suitable husband to be a father to her children, to help raise them and instill positive godly character in them, help pay the bills, and take up part of the responsibility of caring for, spending time with, and disciplining her children, I can't imagine that any single mother would respond with a no. My mother was a single parent, as I said. Even as a child, I understood that a lot of the strain that led to her mental breakdown was the result of her responsibility of caring for three children. And because she was mentally disabled, it was difficult for her to keep employment. In addition, she was too physically drained to keep up with and tend to the needs of all three of us simultaneously.

Same-sex relationships should not be ridiculed and insulted. They are no different from fornication, as no one sin is greater than another (James 2:10). In the end all sexual sins that entail actions contrary to the Bible are often birthed out of a search for love—love that the partakers didn't get at home or love that they never learned to innocently give themselves.

I went looking for love outside of my home, not recognizing that the love I received was very similar to the love that I found at home, until I finally recognized that it wasn't actually love that I was receiving at all. I and my siblings were eventually taken out of our mother's custody and placed in the state's custody because of her mental state, which led to chronic physical abuse and, in some cases, child neglect, often reported by us and school staff. I mention this to underscore the point that the origin of looking for love in unbiblical ways is the need to feel and be loved but having no real reference point or place to honestly relate to real love. Too many of us turned to other means, which can be summed up as desperately looking for love in strange places. *I say this sarcastically.* So, a sexual revolution encore! Sex is free for many, a free-for-all. Free the spirit of perversion with no limits, no boundaries, no shame. Welcome the adulterers, the fornicators, threesomes, and the like! Yes, it sounds interesting, but I wonder if the sexual revolutionaries foresaw all the illegitimate children who would come out of it, the fatherless sons and daughters who are the product of extramarital affairs.

I wonder if the sexual revolution thinkers thought about how these rejected children would be raised in single-parent homes, often living off the government, depending on food vouchers and Section 8 accommodations for free or at a reduced rate of rent as Uncle Sam stands in the gap for the fathers who engaged in sexual revolution behavior but were not willing to take on the responsibility of raising, providing, and caring for the children who were the product of the revolution. I wonder if the revolutionaries considered that these same children would not have an active father at all, or at most have an inconsistent father—or, in a role reversal, have an absent mother who is inconsistent. Parental visits are not the same as having live-in parents. The role of father is so important because fathers provide for and protect their children. How many children are left uncared for financially and emotionally? How many are undisciplined and unprotected because they have an absent or inconsistent father?

Why is it so important to address sin, one may ask? The Bible clearly states that "the wages of sin is death" (Romans 6:23). This doesn't mean that if a person sins, he or she will get hit by a bus thirty minutes later. This simply means that sin in one's life—with the area of our focus being sexual sins—can lead to a disconnected relationship with God because of the resulting shame, regret, guilt, physical disease (AIDS and other STDs), death or loss of one's marriage due to infidelity, severed relationships with one's children because of a coparenting arrangement with a bitter ex-spouse, and so forth. A part of each human being desires to please the very God who created us, so the underlying shame and subconscious knowing that one is outside the will of God can lead to emotional disturbance. The knowledge that something is wrong within, without actually addressing the obvious sin, can lead a person to hide from the presence of God much like Adam and Eve. Hiding from God because of one's disobedience can lead to dodging church attendance or avoiding praying to the Father. Genesis 3:9–13 reads, "And the Lord God called unto Adam, and said unto him, Where art thou? And he said, I heard thy voice in the garden, and I was afraid, because I was naked; and I hid myself." This hiding from God and remaining in bondage can lead to mental stress, shame, guilt, regret, feeling abnormal, and feeling less than acceptable, not to mention the pile-on of rejection experienced in ungodly relationships or the harsh judgment from society, which can lead to the development of depression, anxiety, personality disorders, feelings of worthlessness, and avoidance issues, which in turn can manifest in one's body as physical sickness/illness and disease.

When one harbors rejection after experiencing rejection from another, or when one feels unacceptable or rejected within oneself because of knowingly being outside the will of God, it is very likely that such a person will develop an autoimmune disease or manifest physical sicknesses of all sorts. Many sicknesses and autoimmune diseases begin in the mind when a person believes that they are not good enough or worthy. This, in turn, causes the mind to hate and reject its own body, which is the definition of an autoimmune disease. Instead of the body fighting off foreign infectious cells or viruses, the body begins to turn against itself as it has been trained by the mind to dislike itself by way of the open door of rejection. The body's cells turn against and attack the body through various autoimmune diseases, often stemming from chronic thoughts of rejection taking up residence in the person's bodily functions, expressed as self-hate. Remember, the wages of sin is death. No, you may not ever get hit by a bus, but slowly you are paying the price in your mind, body, and soul for the lack of the peace and safety that is only guaranteed when you live within God's perfect will for your life because you value and love yourself enough to do so. This rejection can be expressed behaviorally through poor self-image, jealousy, comparing yourself to others, or even competing with others for validation, never mind that there is no need to compete because there is not another quite like you!

The role of mother is also important. If a mother is working and going to school yet also raising the children as a single parent, is she really home to advise her children, cook for them, clean for them, or harvest for their future as she should? Those who suffer are the children of the sexual revolution. These same children have little discipline from either parent, with both parents slighting the children even in the best of scenarios. When the parents get married, and after the lust wears off and the regrets settle in, the marriage can be contentious, making it hard to raise a family in such an environment not built on love and satisfaction, which causes the children to suffer in the end. Given all of this, I wonder if the sexual revolutionists considered that unsupervised children starved of attention and love would turn to gangs to be accepted, sell drugs to make up for the lack of two-parent streams of income, engage in carjacking and home invasions, become pregnant as teens, be molested by their mother's boyfriend, engage in promiscuity, drop out of school, and/or use drugs? These children take on a spirit of rebellion much like the spirit they were birthed out of, not being used to consistent discipline, challenging school and community authority, and not having a consistent father figure. All of this leads to treating police like the father who was never there. Therefore, they flee the police or, worse, engage in harm. The sexual revolution has left women broken-spirited and brokenhearted, passing such bitterness and brokenness onto their daughters and sons. Such single parents take on the full role of parenting, thereby denying their full potential to strive and thrive academically or career-wise, not having what is necessary to take the kids to rehearsals to perfect their gifts, provide them with tutoring, help with their schoolwork, or pick them up from school or day care. Absolutely, hats off to the fathers who step up, especially the single fathers or those who stand in the gap to be a father to someone else's child! But from what I gather, what has come out of the sexual revolution is men who have lost sight of what their role is and what is important, and brokenhearted women whose hearts not only are broken by their male counterparts but also were first broken by their absent fathers in their childhood. These women have produced broken-spirited children in some cases. The product, beloved, is brokenness. I was a counselor at a juvenile court, where I saw such cases daily. The children's actions arose from a broken or dysfunctional family system. In addition, I was the product of a father who was missing and broken.

Once one has come to terms with the outcome of one's actions, then one can freely repent. We are at liberty to repent for the collateral damage that we have caused each other, accepting full blame and responsibility. A woman is not at liberty to blame the man if her actions were carried out willingly. We have to repent to our children, repent for not having known better and for lacking in morals, standards, values, and so forth. Once we realize the role we played in this problem, we can forgive the person who hurt us, be it the unfaithful mate, the father who wasn't there, the person with whom we were in a relationship that proved in the end to be unfulfilling, or the mate who didn't value us as we should have been valued. Next it is important to forgive yourself. In forgiving yourself and others, you deny the root of bitterness, which will inevitably materialize if you don't forgive.

Repeat this declaration:

> I forgive the shortcomings of both my mother and father. I employ the help of the Holy Spirit to fill in where my mother, father, and past mates fell short. I forgive all that happened to me as I perceive that it will be revealed in the days to come why it was needful for me to undergo such experiences. I decree that I will regain everything that was lost to me sevenfold. I decree that it will be better than what I had originally envisioned. I trust God with my life. I declare no defeat. I declare that I will win as everything will turn around and work graciously in my and my children's favor. I pray this in Jesus's name. I believe that according to Joel 2:25, Psalm 6:31, and Isaiah 61:7, I will be restored, and I will reclaim a better version of what was lost. I will see my pain become my gain in Jesus's almighty name! I will seek God to restore my life and my relationship with him (Psalm 2:7)!

chapter 5

Open Windows to Unwanted Experiences

Are you embracing certain cultural norms? Were you birthed out of rejection or exposed to abuse or molestation? Open doors are plentiful. They primarily begin in the womb through unwanted pregnancies and generational curses. They are rooted in fear and can connect the dots from the spiritual realm to manifest in the natural realm. Open doors are generally legalized through curses on one's family by engaging in known sin. Known sin is a very common open door. We are to adhere to the commands of the Creator who created us in his image and likeness, meaning that since he is holy, we have a holy compass within us that lets us know that having sex and bearing children before marriage is fornication and cheating on our wife or husband is adultery. But after having engaged in such sin over a period of time, one becomes hard of hearing and finds it difficult to discern the built-in voice of the moral compass and Holy Spirit consciousness. Here is the avenue by which God can turn the individual over to a reprobate mind (Romans 1:27–29).

Sins of perversion, incest, murder, calculated theft, and the like are among many doors of sin that permit the demonic spirits that guide such behaviors and often lead to generational curses. The danger of harboring such spirits is that you can be the victim of one of these spirits or the actual perpetrator of what runs through your bloodline. Both of these avenues can open up a door for generational curses. Certain women have a family history of sexual abuse. The grandparent, parent, and child suffered violations at around the same age committed by men or women who were family members, or friends of the family, or even unknown men or women. Such experiences are the result of the spirit of the victim resting on that generation and thereby unknowingly attracting perpetrators. Have you ever wondered why the same man or woman will attract three domestically violent relationships in a row or why the same woman will attract unfaithful men and have a series of marriages and relationships that all end with the man leaving her for someone he cheated with? The victim spirit has not been ousted from such a lineage, and therefore the majority of those who are afflicted with this spirt attract cheaters, drug users, people who commit acts of domestic violence, men who do not desire to work, women who are less than helpmates, and so forth.

Let's go back. Have you ever thought about what empowers a person to take the life of someone they didn't give birth to (though to take the life of someone they did give birth to is still wrong) and never owned (though to take the life of someone they own is still wrong), and the person was never indebted to them (though to take the life of someone indebted to them is still wrong)? What makes someone kill someone else over $5 worth of drugs or for stepping on a pair of shoes, or because of an argument about a person to whom neither the man nor the woman is married? What empowers them is that they have yielded to the spirit of the action. Such ancient spirits have been killing for decades, stealing for decades, and raping for decades, so they are desensitized to and familiar with the action. Many people are totally unaware that the spirit of murder is even resting on them or their bloodline. This fight is spiritual. The murder spirit is birthed from environments that lack love and that therefore harbor easily kindled anger. Such environments are volatile and dangerous.

Consider Joseph's brothers, who felt unloved and were moved to anger concerning their father's love for and favor toward Joseph. This level of hate and easily triggered anger alone was enough to cause Joseph's brothers to consider killing him, yet they settled for selling him into slavery. The spirit takes over a person's mind who has an open door to it, causing the action to be justified in the moment. And once the action is complete, then guilt, shame, and regret consume the perpetrator as he himself is unable to fully explain the reason for his own behavior.

The effects of this spirit are not limited to acts of perversion and violence but also influence one's health. If spirits of sickness and infirmity, such as that within the woman with the issue of the blood or that within people today who have high blood pressure and overeat, can cause you to steal, kill, and destroy your own health—which is your key life support—slowly yet progressively, then this is just a longer version of suicide, is it not? If the womb that you were incubated in has attached to it the spirit of the victim or the perpetrator of sexual sins, rejection, depression, or something else, then your life can follow a trajectory of that nature. As a result of taking on such spirits without intervention, you may fulfill such a fate in your own life and repeat the cycle, which is the true essence of a generational curse. Those coming from a historical background of slavery have multiple generations of ancestors rooted in rejection because certain slavery situations where ones in which hate, inequality, rape, incest, murder, and superiority/pride were expressed, among other demonic expressions and open doors. Drug use, mental illness, laziness, the tendency to quit, obesity, and low self-esteem are all possible generational curses that work against one's purpose and God-given potential, and people who exhibit these traits also hold the potential to attract a mate who has less than their intended potential as these people themselves are operating below their potential, and like tends to attract like. How many people suffering from obesity find themselves unworthy of the ideal mate they originally had in mind and therefore oftentimes make compromises? How often do both mates engage in self-destructive behaviors such as using drugs? How often do families rooted in laziness and slothfulness suffer from poverty and feel jealousy toward those operating in their God-given calling (Proverbs 10:4)?

A key sign of a generational curse is when the known sin is acceptable and often celebrated in the family. For example, fornication is celebrated by congratulating your cousin that she has a man. And when a child comes out of the continual fornication experience, the family celebrates the birth, having been desensitized to that opened door of fornication. In most cases, emphasis on marriage is never made. Many families don't even call the police when a child has been molested. Instead they have mercy and sympathy for the perpetrator, totally disregarding the emotional support that is necessary for the victim. Most likely these people were abandoned in their own victimization. If it is common within a family to live somewhere and move before the rent is due, overcharging bank cards and never paying the overdraft fees, it is possible that the spirit of poverty is on that family or some of its members. Know that any spirit that is not of the Holy Ghost has been sent only to steal, kill, and destroy (John 10:10)! Of course, demonic doctrines coordinated by the seducing spirits of voodoo, witchcraft, and Jehovah's Witnesses are founded on falsehood or satanism (2 Corinthians 2:5). Such doctrine opens up doors that provide easy access for demons to enter and also give demons access to one's mind, which is their central operating station. This often leads to generational curses and unwanted outcomes. It is critical that we have the necessary knowledge of spiritual open doors so we may be aware and know how to close them, as the Bible tells us clearly that one can perish for lack of knowledge.

chapter 6

The Root of Fear

Fear causes a person to control and manipulate others and not believe in the will of the heavenly Father. People who live in fear therefore place more faith in their own ability than they place in the power and might of the almighty God, who created both heaven and earth. Such unbelief has led many to engage in witchcraft, voodoo, spiritualism, or even seduction to seduce a potential marriage partner, as opposed to obeying God's principles to attract a divine partner sent by God who is based in godly principles. Who better to control heaven and earth than the Creator of it (Genesis 1)? Many people have given in to these seducing doctrines, which are based in self-sabotage, as the principles of these false doctrines are designed by the devil to ensure that what God has intended for the recipient is sabotaged and rerouted, so the situation backfires and the intended party loses what they otherwise would have gained had they waited on and believed wholeheartedly in the Lord, as opposed to their own ability. Fear can lead a person to compromise her standards and therefore lose what God had already originally intended to give her. Adam and Eve had dominion over the earth and were tempted to receive more than what they had lost when they were driven out of the garden. Never give into the temptation to be lord over your own life by rebelling and disregarding the rules and laws of God's Word, as this could cause you to lose the very thing you are compromising yourself to keep.

chapter 7

Forgive to Win

How can you overcome your past to regain your power? So you are married to your past. You're mad at your children's father, who left for another woman. You blame your ex-wife or ex-husband. The woman who got you fired from your last job is the reason for your current lack of money. The dad who molested you or touched you inappropriately is responsible for your current drug use to numb the pain, your current lack of self-worth, and all life's traumas that his abuse helped to create. That man who touched you when you were a young boy has tripped your manhood, and in your promiscuity and confusion, you are fighting to get your manhood back. The physical abuse that you experienced or witnessed in your childhood is the root cause of the domestic violence in your current adult home. Like looking in windows in a Christmas movie, I can see your story. Are you touching your own children or other young children because when you were a child someone touched you? I want you to know right now that whatever is going on in your house, no matter what secret you have kept hidden from other human beings—no matter what it is, my beloved, and

29

whether you are the victim or the abuser, I love you. And God loves you so much that he gave his Son's life for both your sins and mine. No matter what it is, you are no less loved, beloved. Just know that victims and abusers come from the same place. In some cases the victim switches roles, having been abused himself. I find it necessary to tell you again that from the very bottom of my heart, I sincerely love you and I honor you, my brother or sister. I wrap you in my arms, and I cradle your pain away—the pain of the divorce, the pain of the rape, harbored feelings of guilt and shame, whatever it is; some things we won't name here. I am here, and I still believe in you. You are not what you've done or what you've been through. To whomever originally caused that pain in your life, give that pain back right now. You, dear heart, have carried it long enough. It is not your fault! I dry every tear from your eyes right now. I am right there with you, beloved. Trust me. You, my dear, are not alone. Millions of people stand with you. Many men have experienced what you have encountered, and many women have as well.

In counseling, I have heard all the stories mentioned above and some that are too drastic to report and yet are very common. We come from the bottom of the barrel. We are the underdogs. We have been the broken and abused. But I promise you, we are coming out of this to rise to the top and reign!

Beloved, there is a balm in Gilead (Jeremiah 8:22). We read in 2 Kings 5:10–14 an explanation of the healing process of Naaman, a mighty man who was a successful captain of war, yet he suffered with leprosy. The prophet

Elisha instructed him on how to be healed, and the following explains his response:

> And Elisha sent a messenger unto him, saying, Go and wash in Jordan seven times, and thy flesh shall come again to thee, and thou shalt be clean. But Naaman was wroth, and went away, and said, Behold, I thought, He will surely come out to me, and stand, and call on the name of the Lord his God, and strike his hand over the place, and recover the leper. Are not Abana and Pharpar, rivers of Damascus, better than all the waters of Israel? may I not wash in them, and be clean? So he turned and went away in a rage. And his servants came near, and spake unto him, and said, My father, if the prophet had bid thee do some great thing, wouldest thou not have done it? How much rather then, when he saith to thee, Wash, and be clean? Then went he down, and dipped himself seven times in Jordan, according to the saying of the man of God: and his flesh came again like unto the flesh of a little child, and he was clean.

Could it be that the very thing that is stopping you from living the rest of your life to its fullest is something that you view as being beneath you? Like Naaman, you find it too hard to forgive, to release your enemy, to have compassion. I am sure that person's past was not perfect, which unfortunately might have led to them treating you the way they did. Maybe their mother and father wasn't there. Could it be that the person who made you feel broken in a season of your life did what they did to you because they themselves were broken as well? Are you willing to forfeit your healing if it costs you to forgive? No matter how hard it may seem, you must simply forgive those who harmed you.

Naaman was a lot like many men and wo*men* (Naa*man*) are today. Captain Naaman was enraged at the thought of having to dip in dirty water and felt that his cure should come from a clean place such as Abana or Pharpar, the rivers of Damascus. He became enraged and resistant like many of us who misperceive our healing and think that it must come from a place of pure satisfaction, total bliss, or happiness. Many become enraged at the thought that God has called them to a family that has a generational curse so that they may experience the curse and, in so doing, declare Christ and overcome through the blood of the Lamb. Then the words of their testimony may in turn help to deliver others (Revelation 12:11).

Many think that to be a Christian means you live in a perfect castle of peace and eternal bliss. They don't consider the scripture that says, "The Kingdom suffereth violence and the violent take it by force" (Matthew 11:12). Your victory is not always handed to you. Sometimes you have to fight for it, and sometimes the place where you fight for it is a dirty place. Are you like Naaman, despising your muddy Jordan waters, which is the place of your healing? Maybe God allowed you to dip in a dirty place because there you can find the antidote and thereby your cure so that you may be able to share that antidote with others. Captain Naaman's healing was in a dirty place.

Are you bitter or enraged about your healing instructions from heaven because they do not include the cure or a "clean pool," or even a nice, friendly situation, much like Naaman was? Maybe your healing is in a pool of forgiveness or involves overcoming a sickness so that you may witness through your ministry that God is truly the ultimate healer. Maybe your pool to achieving a better marriage is to undergo a temporary separation from your spouse so that God may bring you back together stronger than ever before! Maybe your pool for financial overflow is to trust God with tithing in a dry place so that he may "open you the windows of heaven, and pour you out a blessing, that there shall not be room enough to receive it" (Malachi 3:10). Hear me! My goodness, you prayed for it, but are you willing to dip in the healing pool to receive your breakthrough, much like Naaman?

You are stronger than you know. Who could have encountered all that you have, not only in your early years but also in your adult life, and still strive, still believe, and above all remain standing? For this, beloved, I honor you! I believe in you, and I see your expected end (Jeremiah 29:11). I assure you that all things work together for your good (Romans 8:28). Could it be that God chose you for the particular test you underwent because the process of becoming the cure is first to be injected with the poison? Are you blaming others? Has a root of bitterness and victimization settled within you because you are looking at things all wrong? The scientific field has grasped this concept for various immunizations. It is true that some are injected with a safe, limited amount of the virus to activate their immune system to fight it off. In the event you encounter the actual virus, it hardly has a chance to survive because your body's built-in activated immune system begins working to kill it. Beloved, is bitterness stopping you from becoming the cure? Have you forfeited the chance to be the cure because you have yielded to the poison and lost the immunity, strength, and power to overcome the setback or heartache you encountered so that you may be the resistant force and the antibody not only for yourself but also for your family, your community, and the world.

What are you doing for your inner little boy or girl? How are you loving him or her back to life considering all you've gone through? As you were a victim, others need to hear how you triumphed. Do you not know that there is a little boy or girl out there who has experienced the very same trauma you have, if not worse, and they need to know that someone encountered what they have yet lived through it victoriously? In short, they need your antidote! They need to know your testimony because people overcome by the blood of the Lamb and the words of our testimony! In healing someone else, you are healing your inner self. The little boy or girl in you who was traumatized by what he or she endured needs to be secure, in the protection of your adult self. And more than anything else, by aiding others you establish that you did not encounter that warfare for nothing. Fight the enemy back by helping to rescue another! The security comes from knowing that what happened to you did not hold the potential to break and destroy you or your life's purpose and assignment. The reason for your pain was so that you could take a certain career path, model to your family, display in your ministry, write about in your book and screenplay, and mentor others to be what you have become: the antidote and the cure!

chapter 8

My Testimony

I grew up in a home where my mother was diagnosed with and had clear symptoms of mental illness. My mother named me Romonica. I later came to find out that the name Monica means counselor. My mother birthed the counselor that she needed. I obtained a master's degree in psychological counseling after earning a bachelor's degree in psychology. I became a licensed counselor and have been in this field for over ten years, owning Eclectic Counseling Services LLC, which now has two locations. Looking back, I realize that the environment of mental illness that I grew up in was like a snakebite. Yet in having overcome the trauma of watching my mother's struggle, I have been able to aid countless others who have mental illness through the years. And now I blend therapeutic tools with our faith in God on an international TV show, aiding millions from the comfort of their homes with the leading help of our Lord. To God be all glory!

chapter 9

The Effects

Beloved, now that you have been hurt and even violated, who are you? God asked Adam, "Where are you" (Genesis 3:9)? Might I ask you the same?

Dear heart, where are you? Why are you not in the place of peace, love, forgiveness, healthiness, happiness, wholeness, victory, prosperity, triumph, healing, and fulfillment that God has willed for your life? Why have you sought comfort for your soul in the arms of broken men, broken women, broken people, and broken places? How can your identity be reflected in an individual who doesn't know their own worth or identity, or has not yet overcome their own brokenness, or who has not triumphed over their fractured reality? Why are you so guarded, woman, and why have you become so hard and callous? There is no softness in what should be your feminine nature. You're saying, *No one hurts me because I never let anyone come close enough to be able to hurt me.* But the pain of rejection and abandonment is just as hurtful as having no one pursue you or even trying to get close enough to experience your vulnerability, is it not? Your countenance has changed, and your conversation is far more harsh and judgmental than it should be or would have been had you never experienced that pain. Have you let what happened to you rob you of your femininity or your original loving, caring, giving nature, and as a result do you have trust and relationship problems today? I find that most men don't want to date a masculine-natured woman.

Adam, where are you? Sir, what have you allowed to rob you of your manhood? Though that traumatic experience happened, you can still fight for your manhood. Though your dad didn't set a proper example, you still can fight to be the example. You don't have to stay lost in the garden of life. Beloved, sir, where are you? That woman is expecting you to be a provider, a protector, and a covering for your household. Are you showing up with less than what God expects from you in your male role? Come back today to the place where God has called you victorious. For you are the head and not the tail; you are above and not beneath (Deuteronomy 28:13)! Come take your place of victory, and don't allow what happened to you to triumph over you any longer, beloved! Stand on this scripture: "Behold, I give unto you power to tread on serpents and scorpions, and over all the power of the enemy: and nothing shall by any means hurt you" (Luke 10:19).

chapter 10

The Journey and What to Expect

I f you are going to walk in complete victory in your life, then you must make certain changes. I say complete because many people have some form of victory, but it's not in the area that matters most to them. You may have victory in your family but lack victory in your finances. You may have victory in your ministry or career but have no victory in establishing your family, marriage, or love life. You may have victory in your health or your physical body, but you are severely tormented daily in your mind. If you are battling in any area of your life, beloved, be encouraged, because your subconscious mind has not settled for the conditions of where you are, as the battle in itself is an indication that somewhere you are in a fight for more, for better, for your complete victory! Don't be ashamed that you are battling for your love life, your marriage, higher consciousness, increased finances, better health, wealth, or mental peace. You are fighting because somewhere you have subscribed to the Word of God that says you can live life abundantly and victoriously as "greater works will we do," says Jesus Christ. All that we do in order to have true victory, we must do in his name (John 10:10, 14:12)! I propose to you that the area in your mind in which you are defeated will show up as an area of defeat in your life. Given this, if you are believing for healing in your body, mind, family, or finances, you must first perceive such a thought in a crevice of your mind that God is able and that he will instruct you on how to achieve victory through prayer.

If you perceive it in your mind, then you can do it. The moment you perceive the capability of what you are believing for in your mind, you change the context of your mind, and your mind begins the process of formulating exactly how to do what you are believing God will lead you to do. Jesus asked the lame man, "Do you want to be made whole?" God will not believe for you. You must use your free will to believe for yourself. The desire to want to receive that which you are lacking is a form of faith. To want your finances to improve means that you believe that it can happen. That's faith. It's true: "If ye have faith as a grain of mustard seed, ye shall say unto this mountain, Remove hence to yonder place; and it shall remove; and nothing shall be impossible unto you" (Matthew 17:20). If you don't want it, it may be because you don't believe that it's possible. The cause is often that you have bought into the idea that it's not possible for you.

Why did Jesus ask the lame man, "Do you want to be made whole?" Being made whole is walking in victory in every area of your life, leaving no area untouched. The first question you must ask yourself is whether you want to touch the area of your life that does not have victory and that leaves you unhealed. Does it bother you enough? Is that area of your life too sensitive or too sore for you to address right now? Does it hurt too bad to still believe?

Does the thought of addressing the area of your life that lacks victory devastate you, maybe because you have not healed from the last time that your efforts rendered defeat? Does it hurt because you have not overcome the last heartbreak of having failed in that very area, which has left you unwhole? The heartbreak and soreness is often the result of the impact of the failure, which the deceptive voice of the enemy speaks the lie about, telling you that because that last relationship didn't work out, you're unlovable, or that because you were fired, you're not a provider or a man. If you would allow me, I would love to speak truth and life back into you.

Could it be that the defeat came not because you are any less but because of the means by which you pursued what you were after? Maybe you were attempting to love on your own strength outside the will of God and the holiness of his Word. Maybe you were attempting to love someone else without first coming into the true knowledge of God's love for you, which empowers you to embrace and love yourself so that you have a point of reference to know just how to love another. Maybe the enemy has attacked you in the area of your defeat because he foresees that this will be the very place of your greatest victory! Could the last failure be preparation and life lessons for God's grand finale, for his restoration and breakthrough plan for your life? Now you'll know how to treat the next person, how to be faithful to the next job, how to run that company, how to raise your next set of children, or how to labor for your next ministry. Maybe pride allowed you to think that at your job you could cut corners and not submit to your boss, and on your own strength you lost your job not because you're less than a man but because you attempted to have success on your strength and did not rely on God's will or strength.

One of the hardest lessons I myself learned is the lesson of Zechariah 4:6: "Not by might, nor by power, but by my spirit, saith the Lord of hosts." I had to learn that in the areas that I was believing God for in order to achieve great success, I would have to accomplish victory on his strength and by applying his principles. Many of us attempt to use God's strength for situations where we have failed to apply his principles. How can you pray for the strength of God to turn a situation around when you have engaged in cheating, lying, stealing, fornication, adultery, gossiping, backbiting, witchcraft, control, manipulation, mind games, and the like? Those things are works of the flesh, and when you apply such principles, you are operating on your own strength, which will render utter defeat! You have to break your will and allow the will of God to prevail if you desire to get complete and total victory. If victory is what you seek, then at some point you're going to need the strength of God to carry you through. In battle, you'll also need his authorization, an agreement that bears his signature and permission to obtain what you desire, as anything outside his will, will suffer greatly or be lost. This is because he is the Sustainer—and what can live outside his sustaining powers? If God does not authorize it, don't expect him to back it up. How do you expect him to sign off on a principle that is the total opposite of his holy, righteous, or just nature or his biblical Word? Would you promote an employee who stole from you? Would you increase the allowance of a child who lied to you? Would you hire a treasurer with a proven criminal record of identity theft? Would you encourage your son to marry a known and unrepentant prostitute? Would you place all of your faith in a self-seeking government? Well, how much more do you expect God to utilize the force of heaven in an unrighteous way? To do so would glorify Satan, who is opposed to the true nature and will of God. Why would God open up the door of marriage for someone who is fornicating or lost in promiscuity?

> If you are not putting God first
> before you get married, then why
> should he trust you with marriage?

Yes, many have gone through the door of marriage without God's signature and authorization, and as a result the divorce rate is high. The terrible secrets of many of these marriages involve too much to go into detail about at this time. Trust me, I am a licensed counselor, so I am well aware.

As you are now walking in truth, let's take a look at the lies that the devil told you about your body shape or size, financial status, facial appearance, education, and/ or family background. Maybe there is nothing wrong with you at all. Perhaps it was the method that you used to accomplish what it was that you were believing for. Could it be that you were walking in disobedience of God's Word and therefore it rendered you no favorable results? Obedience is better than sacrifice (1 Samuel 15:22). Don't let the loss make you feel broken. Simply sit back, regroup, and change your strategy to align with the will of God. Then all of heaven will make sure that you succeed in complete and total victory!

chapter 11

What You Feed Will Lead

In order to obtain the victory in the area in which you have gone without victory, you will need to put forth effort. The level of effort that your victory is going to require is often equal to the level at which you have experienced defeat or unbelief. I hear you saying, "What was that?" But why do you think that the area in which you have experienced defeat is unique to you? Do coworkers, neighbors, fellow church members, and family members experience defeat in this same area? The answer to this question is that they do not struggle in the same area in which you previously experienced defeat because their minds are not limited in faith concerning that area, which leaves no room for defeat in their lives. Peter was the only disciple to experience the miracle of walking on water because his mind was not limited to the belief that he couldn't walk on water. Others have accomplished getting married, securing millions of dollars, bearing children, and being healed. They've done this because their minds perceived beyond disbelief, beyond their circumstances, and beyond generational curses in the areas in which they were believing, and this placed them in a definable spot called *faith*!

If you feed yourself marital statistics, the ratio of men to women currently alive on the earth, what happened in your last relationship, or what happened in someone else's marriage that ended in divorce, then you will render the result of defeat in your life because of what you have meditated on. But if you feed yourself the unadulterated, undisputed, undeniable true and living Word of God, it will tear down every mountain of obstacle, every fear, and every uncircumcised philistine of a giant that would dare to stand in the way of your victory (1 Samuel 17:26). Ask yourself, what did other cancer survivors believe? How about those who were miraculously healed of AIDS? What about other women who live in the same world with the same male-to-female ratio as you do and yet are happily married? What did other first-in-their-family college graduates believe? How about remarried individuals? What did successful teenage mothers or single parents believe that lured them from the muck and mire of potential defeat into a place of triumphant victory?

If you are sick in your body, know that by his stripes you are healed. In the area of defeat and shame, know that you shall have double for your shame because your shame qualifies you for double! If you suffer with poverty, know that God is well able to enlarge your territory as "the cattle upon a thousand hills" is the Lord and "the earth is the Lord's and the fullness thereof" (Psalm 50:10, 24:11; 1 Chronicles 4:10). If you struggle with mental illness, know that you have the mind of Christ. If you are ashamed of your past and feel like self-harming because you have been condemned, remember the woman at the well or even the woman caught in adultery, and know that Jesus did not come to condemn either one of them but to set them both free (John 8:11).

For your most hideous hidden secret, Jesus shed his blood for you so you could walk in freedom and go and sin no more. Jesus's love for you led him to the cross so that he may cover your sin by way of the most sufficient sacrifice: his purified shed blood (John 3:16)! Beloved, what you feed will lead. For some victories, you must apply and activate the Word. And some come about through praying and fasting. Fast your way through your healing to find deliverance; pray your way through your doubts and fears; praise your way through trouble; fight your way through battle with the sword of the Word; and dance your way into victory. Then there will be nothing at all that the defeated enemy can do about it! Build on what is working for you, and what you are believing for will certainly come! This is a much better philosophy than rehearsing your failures and shame. Remember not to feed yourself defeat but to rehearse the potential of success, because what you feed will lead. Join a local church and stay rooted and grounded, because without a local church, beloved, you are easy prey and open to demonic attacks (Hebrews 10:25).

Remember: God's principles
equal God's power.

Line up with the Word by bringing your flesh under subjection, and you, beautiful, will *win*!

chapter 12

Forgive and Release to Embrace a New Thing

S trive for better. When you catch the thief called defeat, command it to pay you back times seven (Proverbs 6:31)! Your setback could be a setup for something much greater. Forgive and release. Will you pass the "faith after failure" test so that you may succeed? It will require you to believe despite adversity. I take it that you have had time to digest your appetizer and are now ready for the entrée.

> When you are called to greatness,
> your tests are much greater than the
> average test because your blessings are
> greater than the average blessings.

When you are called to greatness, much like Joseph your faith will be tested. If Joseph had never encountered any trouble, he would have never expanded his faith to the level at which it needed to be for him to walk in his rightful position next to Pharaoh of Egypt (Genesis 41:40). Jesus Christ, the greatest, was tried by the cross.

We know it was a test in that he asked that the bitter cup of having to experience the cross be removed (Genesis 37:5; Luke 22:42). Joseph dreamed that he was superior to his brothers, and his faith that he would overcome the pit, outlast the scandal of Potiphar's wife, and somehow, through the grace of God, make it out of jail proved that he was the measure of man that he appeared to be in the dream that qualified him for his God-given divine position (Genesis 39:7–8). You see, greatness is not a feeling. It is not based on your looks, vanity, your family's last name, your father's anointing, or who your mother wants you to become. Greatness is based on your ability to carry the weight of the glory that will rest on your life—that is, of course, after you have passed the test.

The mother of Zebedee asked for her sons to be seated next to Jesus in heaven. She was asking on behalf of her children as if her desire for this alone would make it possible. Jesus well spoke when he replied that what she was asking for was not his to give but was God the Father's decision to make (Matthew 20:21–23).

The truth of the matter is that if God finds greatness in you from the foundation of the earth, which he has, then he will call you out above your family like Joseph or, in Jesus's case, above all others in the kingdom of heaven. He will call you out and separate you from your family like he did Abraham. He will choose you above other women like he did Esther. He will make your name great as you join the chosen in the Book of Life. "Many are called, but few are chosen" (Matthew 22:14).

You see, you have been looking at that failure all wrong. You thought that because you didn't get the job, because you didn't marry that particular mate, because you didn't have a child the first time you tried, or because you didn't earn the degree that you set out to obtain, the defeat has made you a failure. Yet in all actuality the defeat was beckoning you, calling you out, summonsing you to take a test for a far greater reward. You are expected to use the lesson from your previous test to win!

Out of all the Egyptians who desired to be next to the king in terms of position, Joseph succeeded. How was this possible, seeing as he was not even from their heritage or from their lineage and had a criminal record, having been accused of rape? Look at all the family members and government officials whom Pharaoh could have promoted. But because God called Joseph from the foundation of time, that position was rightfully his. However, he would have never made it to that position had he believed the circumstances of his very first test, that of being hated by his brothers, which he failed. He failed that test greatly. He was favored by his father but was hated by his brothers. What if he would have allowed the so-called failure of ending up in a pit because of his brothers to determine his worth, his future, his value, and the outcome of his life? He used the betrayal of his brothers to pass the test of experiencing betrayal and rejection by those closest to him. He would have forfeited his divinely assigned position of being seated in heavenly places next to Pharaoh in Egypt had he failed this difficult test (Ephesians 2:6). Have you allowed the failure of that job, relationship, or pregnancy test to render you negative results that have shaded your opinion of yourself or even of your future? Have you allowed it to make you feel less than? Well, beloved, it's not the failure that has defeated you; it is your outlook. You believed the failure of your circumstances more than you believe the Word of God concerning your life, as God still has an expected end just for you (Jeremiah 29:11)!

What if Jesus, who was hated by fellow ministers and Pharisees, had believed the words of his haters? Or what if to avoid the consequence of dying on the cross he had bowed down to the enemy's lies about him? He would have lost the faith that he needed to overcome the cross and to rise again on the third day after having taken the keys of the kingdom from Satan and having all power in his hands. Beloved, when did you stop believing the dream that God has given you? What natural circumstance did you deem more trustworthy than the Word of God? Remember, we are to walk by *faith* and not by sight. You see, being great, called, and chosen has nothing to do with your feeling or looking important. It bears a far greater purpose than to stroke your ego or to lace your pride. Sitting in heavenly places and being given large kingdom assignments has to do with, like Esther said, being called to the kingdom—not looking good or making your ex feel less than, but being called to the kingdom for such a time as this. You are called to a great purpose, yet you must not get lost in yourself and think the assignment for your life is about you. Joseph had that dream not for self-seeking purposes but for a cause far greater than himself, which was to preserve the lineage of Jesus Christ. Jesus Christ is the Son of God and the Son of man and could perform miracles, yet he was tried by the cross. And he was crucified not for his own sake but for the sake of humanity, so that none would perish if they believed only in him. What greater cause than for all of humanity's salvation so that we may live both eternally and abundantly (John 10:10)!

Jesus Christ did not let his suffering or even dying on the cross defeat or deter him. He perceived such things as a stepping stone. We read in Matthew 26:64, "Jesus saith unto him, Thou hast said: nevertheless I say unto you, Hereafter shall ye see the Son of man sitting on the right hand of power, and coming in the clouds of heaven." Because his faith carried him through the test of the cross, he prevailed. Truth be told, it is not your looks or anything fleshly that qualifies you to be promoted. It wasn't Esther's eyelashes, makeup artist, or hairstylist; it was her faith and the condition of her heart. I know it was her faith because it was the same faith that allowed her to take a stand for the Jews and to do the work of the Lord that qualified her for the position as queen. I know her heart called her to the position because she was willing to die for the greater cause, declaring, "I perish, I perish" (Esther 4:16)! It was Joseph's faith that allowed him to prevail in the face of adversity, which gave him the ability, without formal education or training, to sustain many nations. It won't be your makeup or body shape, nor will it be where you live, the money you have in the bank, or your good looks that qualifies you to be promoted in the area that you are believing in God for total victory. Your promoter is your connection with heaven through and by faith. But your faith, much like taking a test for school to determine whether you pass or fail, must first be tested.

So the defeat that you suffered was not your final result. You simply made it your

final result when you stopped believing
and took the failure as a final grade.

Don't you know that you can believe God for greater than what you lost? You can believe God past your pits or your cross. You can believe God past the doctor's report. You can believe God past other people voting you out. And if you do in fact believe him, you will be seated in your high position of favor, and with all assuredness you will win and be fully restored.

I speak life today. It is not too late for you to be made whole. You must now take God where you laid the dead thing, the area of defeat and shame, and allow his resurrecting power to resurrect your *faith*, which will, in turn, cause the dead thing to arise!

chapter 13

Why That Test?

You want to go back and get God, but you are a little bit angry or bitter toward him because out of all the tests he could have chosen, he tested you in that area—that one area that you were believing him for, the only thing that you had left, the very thing that you had built your hope and worth on. I hear you asking, "Why did that have to be tested?" You grew up without a family when the only thing you valued was your family. Why did that have to be separated? You always provided and even used your provisional compensation to make up for other areas. Your hair was everything to you. Why did sickness cause it to fall out? Being a mother was all that you had left. Why was that taken away through the death of your child? I hear your heart. You have never been to jail and thereby have defied the odds, not having gone down the road your peers went down, but then you were delinquent in paying child support to a woman you no longer wanted, which caught up with you. Now you have a jail record and are struggling to believe God for a suitable job. You thought that your physical shape would not only get you married but also keep you married, but now you're struggling to recoup after childbirth or taking steroids. You were always the woman who provided for her mate, thinking that providing for him would keep him, but now you are without a job. Why that test?

Breathe. Can I tell you that God did not pick that test? You did. You picked that specific test. As Job said, "The thing that I feared the most came upon me" (Job 3:25).

Let's now put the spaghetti with the meatballs for this amazing entrée. Beloved, if it is your faith that requires you, like Joseph, to obtain your promise, then whatever comes against your faith is coming against your promise. The antithesis of faith is fear. So, what you fear is hindering the faith that you need to receive your promise, thereby opening a door for you to experience contrary encounters. A wise God allows your fear to come upon you so that you may overcome it to close the gaps of fear and solidify your faith, wholeheartedly knowing that you will obtain the necessary faith to possess your promise! If God never tests you in the very area that you fear and that comes against your faith, then you will never reach the level of faith necessary to gain your promise and receive your victory! Where there is no faith, there is no victory.

I know that your fear is based on your test because it is your fear that becomes the instructor who generates your test. But when you let what you fear paralyze you during your test, you get stuck in the wilderness, going around in a circle until you overcome what you fear and until you desire victory far more than you submit to the fear that has set itself before you. Jesus desired our salvation above the wounding of the cross he bore. When your desire to be who God has called you to be is greater than the fearful circumstance that has set itself against your faith, then and only then do you qualify and possess the credentials to be promoted in the area in which you have experienced defeat. You are called to the position of greatness that God has predestined you to hold. If you are disgruntled with your current circumstances, it is quite possible that your subconscious is aware that there is something and someone in you that is far greater than the fear circumstance that you have succumbed to.

Perhaps Joseph, who was highly favored by his father, feared being separated from his father. Therefore, it was only after he overcame the fear of being separated from his father that he realized that God himself would stand in the gap and protect and provide for him greater than his earthly father did. Consequently, when Joseph was second only to the king and had gained his victory, he couldn't credit his father for his victory. He could only glorify God! My goodness, so it's not your job that has provided for you, because God is your provider. It's not your child who gives you worth, as God has deemed you valuable, even enough to die for, before the foundation of the earth (1 Peter 1:20). It's not your looks that give you worth; it is the fruit of the Holy Spirit that adorns you with an inner beauty that shines through your exterior.

Growing up without a family has made you desire one, but your test is to become whole in God first because he is a mother and a father to the motherless and the fatherless, and marriage and children will never fill your inner void, which is something that only God can fill. Are you going to overcome this test and win the victory, or will you let your inner fear, which has taken on flesh and has become your physical test, prevent you from gaining your victory and your blessing?

Yes, the thing that Job feared the most did manifest in his life and came upon him. Yet he refused to allow his deceitful circumstances to defeat his faith in God. Because of this, he was completely restored and made whole, given double what he had lost.

You want to be made whole on your own terms, but it doesn't work that way, as God is Lord. We read in Proverbs 25: "It is the glory of God to conceal a thing: but the honor of kings is to search out a matter." In the area in which you are believing in God for victory, beloved, have you searched the matter out?

Chapter 14

Redefined

One thing to keep in mind is that when you are on the verge of your God-given breakthrough, just about to receive what you desire, whether it is breaking the generational curse of poverty, going on to higher education, or being wed, the enemy will literally ball up his fist and send you every distraction, every challenge, and every gut-wrenching punch that he can muster in the hopes of hurting you bad enough to make you quit, to make you throw in the towel, so that he may keep the territorial grounds demonically influenced if God so allows. During trying times when you must fight the hardest, keep in mind that you are fighting not only for yourself but also so that you may obtain the formula and the bloodline-breaking anointing to remove the yoke of bondage from your family, from your generation, from those whom you will minister and witness to, as the purpose of this test is far greater than just for your breakthrough. You must stand for others. You must open a door of breakthrough for the many who will come after you. They are depending on you in a mighty way. When you are chosen, your favor often comes with this seat inasmuch as favor attracts hate, backlash, and enemies known and unknown. Unfamiliar or family enemies can arise. Hell may seem to have somehow received the memo that you are the warrior who will break the curse and rob the enemy of his freedom to rule and reign over you, your given bloodline, and the many you are called to set free. Therefore, at this time you must be sensitive to God and know that you are not fighting flesh and blood. You are not fighting people but rather the spirit operating in them. You must be sure to be led by Holy Spirit techniques only, making no decisions informed by your flesh. Understand that some demonic spirits come out through fasting and praying, meaning that you must first be delivered from any spiritual hindrances before you can break your bloodline and free your generation by the leading of the Holy Ghost (Zechariah 4:6).

chapter 15

What Got In?

Overcoming the Setbacks in Your Promised Land: Possessing Your Destiny Begins in Your Mind

When you are chosen, you are often hated because to be chosen often comes with special favor and a special anointing and calling on your life that others may envy, not fully grasping the total cost of your call. Every family has that one person who leads the family forward so as to avoid extinction. Just consider if we were all cavemen and cavewomen, unwilling to advance our bloodline. We would have long become extinct. Someone had to decide to leave the caves to go into villages, which eventually led to our modern-day homes. Those indoctrinated in the old family system will fight you, but those family members to come will thank you. Continue to fight against sin, poverty, fornication, fear, bloodline curses, low expectations, and a lack of education to get your family to their intended promised land. However, in order to accomplish this, you yourself must be free of the bloodline's spiritual hindrances that you are freeing your family from. Given this, it is quite possible that the very curse you are attempting to break will challenge you as a means to overtake you in an effort to subdue your victory.

How can Satan cast out Satan (Matthew 12:27)? The Word says that these curses come out by fasting and praying. It is important that we fast and pray, meditate on God's Word, lay prostrate before God, and utilize the fruits of the Spirit in our interactions with others, as all such warfare weapons will aid in self-deliverance and help us maintain positive relationships with those who will fight the anointing on our lives out of their unwillingness to be delivered by the God-given call on our lives. In the midst of your territorial warfare, which also breaks bloodline curses, stay completely sensitive to the Holy Spirit as he will tell you when to speak, when to be silent, when to show up, when to show out, and when to remain calm. In spiritual warfare, he is your commander in chief.

There are times when you have to meet force with force, and there are also times when you must realize that the purpose of the attack is to perfect your character, meaning you are to "humble yourselves therefore under the mighty hand of God, that he may exalt you in due time" (1 Peter 5:6). After such times, you must know when the season is up, lest you remain there too long in warfare and miss your time of mighty breakthrough. During this period of warfare, fear *must not* be an option, because demonic forces feed off of fear, the same fear, in fact, that they have of you because of the God-called assignment placed on your life to come mightily against hell's kingdom! Fear brings about terror. If you encounter any fear or terror, know that it is a sure sign that you are losing the terr(or) itory of your promised land. the degree of your warfare is equal to or greater than the degree of your breakthrough. Understand all the while that your breakthrough is sure and written in heaven's records, so you will be neither denied nor delayed. Amen. Pursue all and seek God, and "having done all to stand, stand therefore," knowing full well that whatever wall that has set itself before you has no other option but to fall because the Great One is inside you (Ephesians 6:13–14; 1 John 4:4).

You have the advantage. You are the chosen one of God, and your warfare is a setup to bring you overwhelming victory and to cause you to gain the necessary wisdom for your set place.

chapter 16

Don't Lose Yourself

L et's talk relationships, if your promised land or territory is marriage—though this material can apply to other areas as well. Anyone you serve without the wisdom of God as though they are an idol will not become your set husband or wife or may not be with you permanently because God is a very jealous God. When something or someone is an idol to you, you don't bear the weight to be their equal, meaning that you lack the ability to bring balance to the relationship in the area of holding them accountable, aiding them to be in alignment with the will of God for their lives, setting and establishing healthy rules and boundaries that will govern their soul, and achieving wellness in the relationship with both of you maintaining your overall well-being. This applies to personal relationships, parenting relationships, and mentoring relationships. Please target the area of your life to which this best applies.

When you lack a proper independent identity, you lose yourself in your mate or otherwise merge your identity with his, thereby losing your identity, meaning that you become a mimicking reflection of him. As a result, he is now in a relationship with himself because your balanced presence does not exist. Right here your relationship is in trouble, and your partner will certainly look for a whole individual who can balance him out, as the goal of marriage to a woman is for her to be a helpmate. How can you be a reflective helpmate if your identity is dissolved in your mate's and therefore you have no ability to challenge him in areas where he needs strengthening in a loving way that will safeguard him and the relationship? Being a wife in this way is like driving a car with no rubber on the tires in that your independent presence is not there to buffer or balance the trajectory of the relationship or to aid your spouse in becoming his better self to ensure he reaches his God-given destiny. God gave men and women our identity in Genesis, noting that we were made in his image. So our identity is the cornerstone of our careers, parenting, relationships, and marriage and of everything we do.

If you lose your identity as an individual by immersing yourself in your children, in your ministry, or in your career, you also lose yourself and your way. You are now no longer an asset but a person who is desperate for love to such a degree that you are willing to lose your own identity. Self-love is nonexistent at this point. You are no longer a helpmate but a liability as the relationship is now missing a person, namely, you! God discussed man's image and identity before he created man or woman. This is an indication that the most powerful part of you is who you are and what you uniquely represent as a person (Genesis 1:26). What is important to you? What all has crafted how you think, move, and act; your heart's desires; and your gifts and talents? When you lose your identity, you have lost your most valuable part as your identity is in essence connected to your worth, value, and meaningfulness. It is the most precious part of you. That's why Satan challenged Jesus Christ's identity by saying, "If thou be the Son of God, cast thyself down: for it is written, He shall give his angels charge concerning thee" (Matthew 4:6; Luke 4:9). If only Satan could have made Jesus doubt who he was, that would have caused him to abort his assignment, having lost the authority of his identity, which was needed to carry his assignment to completion. We are forever grateful that Jesus passed the identity test and stood on who he was, answering, "It is written again, Thou shalt not tempt the Lord thy God" (Matthew 4:6–7). Have you lost your identity and your value and traveled off the course of completing your assignment? And as a result, do you look for love in an individual whom you already have readily and easily available to you in the pure love of our Father?

If so, then hugs from me to you, but let's ask the hard questions! Women and men, may I ask you, as God asked Adam, "Where are you" (Genesis 3:9)? You should be established in your finances, your education, and your own goals and dreams long before you are equipped mentally and experientially to be able to fully succeed in doing life with another.

Ruth worked in Boaz's field before they got married. She was able to suggest to him how to till it and then to expand that advisory role after marriage to be a suitable helpmate. Imagine if she had never worked and had waited for a man to "save" her. What valuable feedback could she have provided to Boaz as a solid helpmate?

Having your own identity is the equivalent of being whole, the root word of which is *holiness*, meaning that you are whole enough to stand on God's holy principles, above those of any fleshly desires of your own or your mate's. By achieving wholeness is how you learn to be whole enough and complete in the things of God so you don't have to compromise your body, or your standards or principles, to be with someone else.

You will soon learn that God rewards righteousness with riches. "I have never seen the righteous forsaken nor its seed begging bread" (Psalm 37:25).

chapter 17

Childhood

I t is imperative that we acknowledge the conditions of our childhood when we evaluate the quality of our adult lives. Many of us were not raised with a father in our lives and therefore were lacking in the display of manhood. It is also quite possible that our mother did not set a healthy standard of womanhood either. In such cases it is possible that we have searched for the love that we did not receive routinely from our parents in others. Know that when this occurs, you are often looking for a love for which you have no foundational example. Here is where your standards can be far lower than what God intended for you.

Because of the rejection or abandonment that you experienced in your childhood, you may now be attracting relationships of rejection and abandonment. If you witnessed domestic violence at home, it is likely that you will attract control-based relationships. At the center of control is fear, and we know that perfect love casts out fear. You may be in a relationship centered in love, but quite likely you are serving a need as opposed to a loving desire or want. If your father was not in your life, it is possible that you will be attracted to those who are uncommitted, seeing that making a commitment was not an example that your father set or established in your life. If you witnessed alcoholism and drug use in your home, it is likely that you grew up around addicts, in which case you also witnessed an enabler. If you find yourself in return being addicted to drugs, being abusive, being a cheater, being a nonprovider, or enabling a mate who has such traits, know that this behavior was learned. Many people find their purpose in enabling their loved ones. This is the reverse of control. It is possible that you are enabling your loved ones because you fear that if they were sober, healthy-minded, whole, a provider, and so forth, they would not choose you.

Love does not enable. It seeks the best for others. For example, would you enable your five-year-old son not to attend preschool? Would you enable your three-year-old daughter not to learn how to walk? Would you enable your college student granddaughter not to learn how to drive? When we enable others, we make them dependent on us, meaning that they serve the purpose of making us feel needed, in which case what we are giving them is not love at all. Instead we are soothing our need for control to ensure their continual presence in our lives. Does that sound like you? In searching for the love you did not receive from your parents, you may find that this desperation can cost you your entire life. To produce children with someone unmarried or unloved has the capacity to change your entire life, including your future goals, all because you are seeking to fulfill the goal of feeling loved. You engage in premarital sex or hope to produce a child to receive the love from someone that you didn't receive from others.

The level to which you are willing to go and risk obeying God's will and Word to obtain love is equal to the degree by which your need for love has become desperate. Nothing should be more important than attaining your God-given set purpose. When a person becomes desperate to find love, it indicates that the need for love has completely taken over their life. They can see no other need but the desperate need to be loved by all the wrong people. This is how more children are raised without fathers, perpetuating the cycle, as one settles for becoming a baby's mother or a baby's father—and in some cases one of many. You often lose your identity in looking for the love in others that is available to you, even in your ability to love by caring for and catering to yourself.

Have you lost who you were created to become— perhaps a teacher (like my mom), a preacher, a lawyer, a hairstylist, a lawn care technician, or a dentist—all because you have been searching for love, which oftentimes leaves you empty because you tend to attract your own qualities in a mate or the wrong mate when you are not healed and whole? If you are unloved and at risk of losing all that God created you to be, you oftentimes attract another person who is lacking self-love and, therefore, also lacking the ability to love you. The Bible instructs us: "Love thy neighbor as thyself" (Matthew 22:39). Even here we are not obliged to love another beyond our ability to love ourselves. If you attract a mate who does not value or love themselves, how then are they able to love you, beloved? Perhaps growing up you were sexually abused. Because your physical body has natural responses, it is quite possible that you, having experienced sexual abuse as a child, have found that the use of your body is the key thing you use to express love to others. Please be advised that this is considered perverted love, as our example of love is set by our heavenly Father.

"For God so loved the world, that he gave his only begotten Son" (John 3:16). Here we see that real love is not sex based, beloved. Perverted love can be a reference point of promiscuity, homosexuality, prostitution, and loose boundaries, which includes not being willing to wait, not saving yourself for marriage, or not adequately getting to know a person before giving yourself to him or her in a sexual way. This type of behavior, of course, is not safe. It can lead to STDs, emotional attachments, and soul ties and is the exact opposite way that God set for you to obtain and birth the marriage he has intended for you, which is far more spiritually based than it is flesh or lust based. In the garden of Eden, Adam never penetrated Eve's body, yet he knew her by the spirit, and they were husband and wife. Their relationship was not sex based, yet they fulfilled a purpose together and worked together. Adam sacrificed his obedience to God, his Creator, to follow Eve in sin/disobedience (Genesis 3:6). Maybe this fallen state of relationships began back in the garden, as we can see it did not work for Adam and Eve. Have you been operating your relationships from a fallen perspective and point of view? If so, how is this working for you? We certainly don't have to repeat our forebearers' mistakes. Instead we can learn from them.

Lust takes. It is selfish and often does not commit. Lust in itself does not last past the point of immediate gratification. In the example that our heavenly Father set, we see that to love is to place others before oneself. "Love gives, sacrifices, is kind, thinks no evil, does not puff up, is longsuffering, does not envy, is not self-seeking, bears all things, believes all things, hopes all things, endures all things and is not easily provoked" (1 Corinthians 13:4–7). Many have missed their God-given husbands and wives because they have indulged prematurely or with the wrong person in lust. Here is where the importance of loving yourself comes into play. The love that you give and sow in others is the same as, if not greater than, the love that you must come to learn to give yourself. In pursuit of this aim, you should do what you enjoy with someone or preferably alone since self-love centers around oneself. This means that you should cater to yourself. Take yourself out to eat, to the nail parlor, to the movies, to play sports, or to a picnic with a self-made lunch; read your favorite book; run a bath to unwind; play your favorite music; invest in your gifts and talents; or sit down with your favorite drink (hot tea, hot chocolate, or well-made coffee) and reflect on your day, write out your goals, and see yourself living abundantly and victoriously! If you ever feel alone, the "Holy Spirit will comfort you," and God will send you sincere people to help build you up to perfect you for your soon-to-arrive queen or king (John 14:26)!

Invest in your own future, education, and career. Mentor classes, buy real estate, take computer classes, write your book, brand yourself, go for the audition, join the group, forgive yourself, build yourself up, lose the weight, and define yourself as lovable and handsome or beautiful. Ignore societal standards of success. Be grateful you've come this far. Celebrate yourself and the fact that you are still standing. Treat yourself; you deserve it. Lose the weight that has been weighing down your positive self-image, lose negative friends and unsupportive enemies, value your opinion over the opinions of others, lose the baggage by forgiving others, envision something greater for yourself, and see yourself recovering all. Just give yourself permission to be great!

Forgive yourself of the mistakes that you made and the time that you wasted. God can and will restore your years (Joel 2:25).

Embrace and accept the parts of you that others have hated, rejected, or talked about. Embrace the parts of you that you look down on. Perhaps you didn't graduate from high school. You may not know how to read. Maybe you became a teen parent. Perhaps you did not graduate from college. Possibly there are other standards that you didn't meet. Maybe you're currently unemployed. Maybe you have been incarcerated or have done things you regret. Whatever the case may be, forgive yourself and embrace yourself as God's grace and mercy is sufficient for you (2 Corinthians 12:9). God's Son Jesus Christ died on the cross for your sins and shortcomings and he bore your shame, so there is nothing that you should carry from your mistakes, as Jesus has carried that cross for you (Isaiah 53:4–5). Intentionally love yourself where others would not. Intentionally love the parts of you that you once disliked. Embrace your outer person. Intentionally review where the self-hate took root, whether it arose because of the negative words from someone you looked up to, your parents' preference for another sibling over you, another sibling's having a father present while yours wasn't, or feeling as though others' gifts and talents were more valuable than yours. Self-love is key so that you can have the proper standards of what true love is and avoid relationships of domestic violence, chronic unrepentant infidelity, extreme verbal and emotional abuse, and deep issues of control that change how you see and value yourself, thereby altering your destiny and ability to perform to reach your expected end.

Self-love is knowing you don't have to earn someone's love. You don't have to make them accept or love you. You are just perfect as you are naturally. It is your natural self that will attract the right mate for you, the right job, the right advancement, the right promotion. Your life will line up with who you are naturally.

Who would you be had you not encountered all the negative things you have endured in your life? Do the day-to-day work by spending time with God to be remade in his image. Become who he already created you to be. He created you beautiful, successful, and intelligent and gave you all that is necessary from the onset. If you do not like where you are, just know that you are not who you have become. There is something much greater in you. The danger is that the rejection that you have experienced by self or others often causes you to alter who you naturally are, alter what you were created to do or be, and alter what you think you deserve, and therefore you settle for less in your quality of life, relationships, expectations, finances, etc. Self-love involves seeing yourself as God sees you, the perfect image in which he created you, because the way you see yourself and the inner potential you believe exists within you is absolutely true! Never second-guess yourself, because if you believe something in your heart, so it is (Proverbs 23:7). Allow God to heal you. Be assured that Jesus himself would die on the cross all over again just for you; he loves you that much. Spend time with God in his Word, praise and worship him, and set your face and affection toward him so that he may heal you where you are broken. Jesus himself is the healer. Get to know him deeper and hear what he says about you as opposed to conforming to society's standards, your ex's opinion, your parents' opinion, your enemies' opinion, or, as with Joseph, even your jealous siblings' opinion. Hear the Father concerning you!

chapter 18

Hate in the House—Sibling Rivalry

Many of us have encountered haters. The question is, where do haters come from, and in which environments are they produced? I as a counselor have found that many have learned to hate others in the environments in which they grew up. Many learned how to talk poorly about each other, reject one another, and practice unsupportive competition-based behaviors in the privacy of their own homes long before they became the haters we encountered outside their homes. Hate in the household is most common in the display of sibling rivalry. Sibling rivalry can come into existence through a parent's expression of favoritism, as was the case with Joseph and his brothers. Sibling rivalry can also come through critical self-observation. Some siblings are more gifted, smarter, more attractive, and more well-rounded and have more social skills and possibly a more desirable calling on their lives than other siblings. Such appeared to be the case in many ways for Joseph. In the case where you are blessed to have a gifted sibling, your goal should be to glean from them, learn from them, and cover and protect them.

Consider that God trusted you enough to cover, protect, and pray for his chosen vessel. You, therefore, are chosen as well. To know God trusts you is an honor in that you know surely that you have something to offer for God to have put you in such close proximity to his chosen vessel. More often than not, a sibling in your position has something to offer the chosen vessel so that he or she may learn from, glean from, and cover you in return. In cases like this, know that no one has your personality or your gift, no one speaks like you or thinks like you, and no one is gifted in the particular area in which you are gifted; therefore, you have no competitors. You are God's original, and don't you ever forget it!

Jesus Christ's half-sibling preached the gospel and followed in Jesus's footsteps. What an honor it was for him to be a sibling to Jesus Christ. God could have chosen anyone, but he trusted James with the task (Galatians 1:19). What a privilege the members of the Jackson family have to be related to one another. What is your perspective on how you see being a sibling of one of God's chosen vessels? I believe you should consider yourself chosen as well! It is quite difficult to live in the house with someone whose appearance is more socially acceptable or who possesses the confidence or characteristics that you desire. Often people do not consider the possibility that their sibling's attributes only exist because of the purposed assignment to which God himself has called the sibling to fulfill. Every gift that a person possesses is an indication of the purpose that God has created for them to fulfill. If your younger brother is naturally a good teacher, he may be called to teach. If your eldest sister is a great singer, have you considered that she may be called by God to praise and worship him through song? If your baby sister is a beauty queen, could it be that she is drawn to beauty pageants because she has a divine purpose to reach a destiny and not by chance? Considering these things, how unfair is it to have hate in the household or in your heart, where you hates your brother's natural teaching ability or your eldest sister's singing ability? And how unfair it is for you as a sibling to hate your baby's sister natural beauty? None of these attributes are things that these gifted siblings created themselves.

Is it not God who creates us and, therefore, gifts us to do what he has called and created us to do? We must consider whom we are mad at: the gifted individual or God, the latter of whom gave the gifts and entrusted our siblings with those gifts so that he may be edified (James 1:17).

It is the enemy's will to place a talented, gifted, God-called individual in a household with a sibling who suffers from feelings of inferiority, competiveness, and low self-esteem so that the sibling called by God, whose sibling has been entrusted to cover him or her, if led by Satan, will criticize and reject the sibling and attempt to break his or her confidence in a false attempt to build himself or herself up, which in return only makes him or her look small and feel even smaller for having done so. Breaking down another individual because one finds oneself lacking in comparison is certainly not of God (2 Corinthians 10:12). The power you put into pulling someone down, if wisdom were to be applied, could be used to build yourself up, beloved. It is wise for the sibling who suffers by comparison to begin to explore their gifts, natural talents, purpose-filled call, social, emotional, physical, and spiritual needs, and uniqueness.

By strengthening oneself and focusing inwardly, one can become the best version of oneself, which will bring about fulfillment and inner satisfaction, which should cause the self-hate to subside with the hope of minimizing the individual's expressing hate toward others. It is often possible that those whom we live in the home with are used by God to prepare us for our God-given call or for the rejection of haters we may face while on our journey to success in the world outside our homes. Consider this: if you have overcome family rejection, then the rejection of coworkers, in-laws, critics, colleagues, supervisors, and others is easier to overcome to ensure your victory. Joseph could easily forgive Potiphar's wife, having been betrayed by his siblings long before he ever encountered her (Genesis 39:7–20). I hope you have come to celebrate the gifting of those around you, especially those in your family, as their gifts have the potential to break bloodline generational curses, which in turn can open up doors for you, my love. In addition, I hope you have come to realize that the apple doesn't fall too far from the tree, meaning that if your siblings are gifted, then you, if you look in the mirror, will realize that you are also gifted and talented and have natural abilities that match your God call as well. In realizing those gifts connected to our identity, it gives us all the ability to overcome the temptation to become insecure or to feel inferior just because our gifts are different from those of our siblings. Comparing yourself to a sibling, or to anyone else for that matter, can breed insecurity and low self-esteem that can affect your love relationships, lead you to settle for less, and affect the way you raise your children with repeated cycles of low self-esteem and low expectations. Or it can breed depression, anxiety, and feelings of unfulfillment and insufficiency to complete the task that God has called you to, purposed you for, and created just for you. Let's resist and overcome hate in and outside the house of our hearts today!

chapter 19

Self-Love over Mental Illness

Growing up without love in one's life, especially during childhood, which are the formative years and therefore critical to one's overall mental, physical, and emotional development, affects every area of one's life. Many have not drawn a connection between these two things. Love is a basic emotional necessity and a natural desire; therefore, it is quite natural to desire to love and be loved. We often are jaded by a lack of love, so much so that after we have suffered a breakup or rejection, we put on a false persona as though we don't need love or don't need a mate. Denying love, which is a natural part of life, is often an unconscious outcry, making it that much more obvious that the person is in need of what they are missing or lacking: love.

As a counselor, I have found that denial is dangerous. When a person is in denial of their desire to love and be loved, they end up making irrational decisions. You can beat yourself up internally by blaming yourself for not being perfect or internalizing regrets after a failed relationship or failed attempt to acquire love. Internalizing rejection can lead to self-hate, eating disorders, depression, suicidal thoughts, aborted destinies, feelings of worthlessness, and other misfortunes. Rejection can be delivered at the hands of a mate, parent, child, or sibling or by a person you admire or look up to. Understand that rejection is the opposite of love; therefore, it is clearly hate.

> You never reject what you love, and
> you don't accept what you hate!

When we deny the fact that we as human beings naturally require love, we fail to realize that God attempted to meet this human need, not only through his love for us but also through providing us with two parents and a family to ensure the right support and, more importantly, the love needed to make us into whole, well-rounded individuals. We must remember that love is critical. That is why the enemy fights against love, families, and unity to the degree that he does (Matthew 24:12). Love is required to accomplish hard tasks. Jackie Robinson was able to weather the hatred of racism because he had a loving wife and family around him, among others. The hate he endured in the course of his career was counteracted by his warm and loving family embrace. The same was true for Martin Luther King Jr. Jesus Christ was able to bear the weight of the hate that came with the cross because of the assured love that he obtained from his heavenly Father God, who expressed, "This is my beloved Son, in whom I am well pleased" (Matthew 17:5). God's love overpowered and replaced the hate and rejection Jesus Christ received from the world, making the cross bearable. In order for one to pour out properly, one must be properly filled. How could Jesus give his life out of his sincere, pure, and genuine love for us unless first the empty place inside him was filled with the love of the Father so that we may receive the overflow of that love?

Are you giving love from a desperate, thirsty, or dry place? If so, what you are giving is not sincere, pure, and genuine love, beloved. Love is an anchor when the world tells you that you're not cute enough, skinny enough, smart enough, gifted enough, educated enough, or light-complexioned enough; that you don't have the right last name; or that people like you shouldn't expect to succeed. Love anchors and neutralizes hate, making you all the more unstoppable, believing not the opinion of the world but taking on the true identity and love of our heavenly Father to overcome like Jesus Christ overcame earthly rejection. When we do not come to know the full and true love of our heavenly Father as Jesus did, we compromise our values with a spouse and therefore lower our expectations and lessen our chances for marriage, minimize our parenting so as to be accepted by our children, compete with our siblings for parental affirmations, criticize others to build ourselves up as though the individual to whom we are comparing ourselves is the standard, and engaging in self-sabotage. We must come to realize that we are already loved more than we could ever imagine by our children, parents, and heavenly Father. Just look around and see that there are far more around you who love you than the few who reject you (2 Kings 6:16). Have you ever considered that the few who reject you, compared to those who embrace you, do so out of their inability to see their own worth, leaving them completely blind to the ability to see yours? Love is powerful. If you don't obtain it from those you expect it from, simply look up as Jesus did and obtain love from your heavenly Father. See what he says about you as you are fearfully and wonderfully made in the image of God himself, the Creator of both heaven and earth (Psalm 139:14)! Even more, always know that Jesus Christ would die on the cross all over again specifically for you because you are just that special and loved by him.

Beloved, you are loved far more than you could ever imagine! Reach up and just grab it. Feel the love of God and his ministering angels surrounding you, keeping you, protecting you, providing for you, and standing for you. It's all things you, beloved! When a person has experienced a drought of love in their life due to unfortunate circumstances, they may find themselves in unloving relationships rooted in verbal, physical, financial, and emotional abuse, which they accept out of their desperation to fulfill a natural need, namely the need for love, having no real example of what real love looks like. Parents often think that because they have provided for a child, that is love. Our federal government provides housing and food vouchers for many. I wonder if the recipients of those benefits ever feel real, tangible love from their government. Sacrifice is love, yet providing is a basic necessity and does not always translate into the recipient feeling loved. Love is often expressed through spending time, showing support, building a person up, and showing care, interest, and concern. Love is forgiving, displaying grace, encouraging a person to be their highest and best self, believing in a person, encouraging them, being gentle, being kind, being patient, being protective, being understanding, helping someone where they are limited, helping someone overcome, hearing people out, investing who you are, and giving of your resources to another person without holding back. Love takes pleasure in meeting others' emotional needs, discussing their day, investing in their talents, spending quality time with them, building on their strengths, and taking every opportunity to meet their needs and desires without reservation. What your father never told you and your mother never knew about love is that providing alone is a basic, fundamental, primitive requirement, and just because other fathers and mothers do not provide, that doesn't give anyone the right to feel that providing is anything more than just basic. Truthfully, animals care for their young. Dogs provide their milk, birds provide a safe nest, and elephants are protective of their calves and afford them milk. As humans, our capacity to receive and to give love is far greater as our intellect and intuitiveness provides us a more advanced experience. So when a person does not have a human example of true love, they often attract the rejection that they are accustomed to, not because they are deserving of it but because it is an emotional environment they are familiar with. There is no justifiable reason for you to suffer chronic infidelity, a lack of commitment, or a void from being neglected in the area that matters to you the most.

Case in point: there are some medical problems that doctors cannot trace because there is no physical ailment that is treatable or even detectable as the cause of the experienced illness. For example, why would a quality beautiful woman marry a man who she knows is not faithful? Could it be because she witnessed her mother being in unfaithful relationships, and as a result, the spirit of rejection attached to her through exposure? Why would an intelligent student who is smart enough to graduate be too afraid to take her state board test in order to practice? Could it be that she has been called stupid by family members growing up? What is causing you to be in cyclical relationships that end in no permanent commitment, leaving you to have to compete for love? Why haven't you opened the business or filled out the application to further your education? Why are you in a dead-end relationship that's not worth discussing with friends and family? Why are you allowing your children to disrespect you? Why are you in friendships that highlight your failures and continually downplay your strengths? Why are you attracted to rejection? Could it be because such toxicity resembles the family that you grew up in or just your inner thoughts concerning how you truly feel about yourself?

You are loving, giving, and attractive. You have all the attributes that the right man or woman desires. Could it be that the spirit of rejection, barring no physical reason to justify your choice of unloving relationships, is common to you because, even though you have everything one could hope for physically and emotionally in a mate—and, yes, you are smart enough to pass the state boards—has manifested as either others rejecting you or you rejecting yourself. Has this now become a spiritual problem? Do you carry a spirit of rejection possibly passed down from your parents or that entered you through a lie you believed about yourself because of an experience you went through? When a person carries a spirit of rejection, the spirit of rejection within them will often attract the very same spirit of rejection in mates, friends, and so forth, as spirits attract like spirits.

Leah looked to Jacob to be accepted, devoting her life to gain his love and affections. If she would have looked upon the acceptance of her heavenly Father, who thought enough of her to choose her to help birth Judah, the patriarch of the tribe into which his divine Son Jesus would be born, how much more beautiful her countenance of confidence and self-esteem would have been, which by nature would have naturally drawn Jacob to her or even provided her with fulfillment on the inside, which is of far greater value than the attention of a man. Don't forget, as a woman you are purposed to reproduce. Keep in mind that African Americans have a history of abuse translated as rejection, which might be the thing responsible for cultural habits of rejecting one another more often than supporting one another. This behavior is considered learned. You may find yourself in toxic relationships because you do not love yourself. Your love for yourself should not be based on your accomplishments, weight, size, annual salary, education, or any other performance-based measure, as Jesus did not die for just the beautiful or the educated. He died for us all!

When you do not love yourself and when you have not have received the readily available love of God, you participate in highly toxic relationships that are counterproductive to your overall mental, emotional, and physical health and even spiritual well-being. Such counterproductiveness is common in verbally, physically, and emotionally abusive relationships, which can lead to devastating events such as a divorce after thirty years of marriage because of infidelity, including infidelity with the other spouse's family member or best friend, untrustworthiness with family assets, and discovery of child molestation experienced in the home. Such traumas are commonly heard of in counseling and can devastate the victim's mental state, often leading to mental illness, suicide attempts or ideation, depression, homicidal attempts or ideation, and yes, mental breakdowns.

When you know it's raining, you grab an umbrella or a raincoat to protect yourself from the harsh weather conditions. Such is life. When you love yourself, you protect yourself from the harsh world by guarding your heart, your time, and yourself from those who do not love, value, and pour into you (Proverbs 4:23). You protect yourself with standards, expectations, requirements, and knowing your worth. However, when you do not know what love is, you go into a harsh, cold, and cruel world unprotected, open to the harshness of the world's elements of abuse, rejection, and misuse. Loving yourself is like an umbrella in a rainstorm; it will protect you from certain relationships that are counterproductive to your destiny and mental health. When you love yourself, you avoid relationships with people who do not equally love you as Christ loves the church (Ephesians 5:25).

chapter 20

You Are One of a Kind

Through social media outlets, music videos, siblings, coworkers, and our easily accessible interactions with the many people around us, it is very easy to place focus on the positive attributes of others while in turn losing focus on our own giftings, callings, and blessings. With so many interactions with others and with accessibility to the lives of others and a window onto their success, it is easy for us to take our focus off ourselves. In a world where the focus becomes what others have or are doing, who is married versus single, or who has children versus who is waiting to give birth, it is our responsibility to celebrate the successes of others but to place primary emphasis on what God himself is doing in, through, and by us (Romans 12:15). We must realize that we are certainly not replaceable and that the call on our life and the destiny and purpose that God has for us cannot compare to what is taking place in the life of another. If our key focus becomes on what others are doing, then we tend to focus more on those whom we know limitedly through social media or TV and less on those closest to us. When we focus primarily on others, we lose self-esteem, a sense of self-value, and a sense of self-worth because we are minimizing the key role we play in this world holistically and for the benefit of those around us.

You must strive to thrive despite your naysayers because you believe in yourself and I believe in you! When we abort our God-given authority and abandon our God-given position to place emphasis on another's life, we starve our very own destiny with neglect and abandonment. Over a given period, this leads to spiritual abortions or miscarriages. Could this be why you have not birthed that ministry, opened the shop, or gone back to school?

Hear me: in coveting another person's life and position, you lose your identity, you lose your calling, you lose sight of who you are, and even more, you lose what you were specifically created to do or produce (Exodus 20:17). This is counterproductive as you will never advance in someone else's lane, purpose, call, or God-chosen life. When you become obsessed with the life of another, you are fighting a losing battle that you are neither equipped nor designed to win. The person you admire is who they are, and you, dearly beloved, are who God created you in essence to be. It is critical that you not waste any more time and begin to shift your focus onto perfecting where you are and where you are going so God can bless you according to your obedience (1 Samuel 15:22).

Focusing on others leads to competitive behaviors, as was the case for Cain and Abel. Cain focused on Abel's sacrifice and killed him when he discovered that his own sacrifice did not measure up. Out of jealousy, which is a common denominator of such counterproductive behavior, Cain killed his sibling and thereby aborted his own destiny as he was marked with death and driven out of his current location (Genesis 4:1–15).

Has jealousy caused you to murder someone's reputation, destroy their key relationships, speak ill of them in an attempt to destroy their self-image, come against their ministry, or speak against their success? And in return for trying to destroy another person, what harvest have you reaped in your own life? Like Cain, by sowing destruction, you can reap the harvest of death (Galatians 6:7–8).

Saul envied King David and, because of this, attempted to kill him on several occasions. In the end, King Saul reaped that selfsame harvest by dying on his own sword. He even led his son Johnathan to a premature death. When you covet God's purpose for another person's life, you are feeding sudden death to your own would-be harvest. Focusing on the blessings of others is a very dangerous area. Tread with much caution, or better yet, avoid doing this at all costs (1 Samuel 18:11, 19:1, 31:1–4).

In addition, consider how the dysfunction arising from coveting the lives of others displayed in front of your children can create a generational cycle of failure because of the distractive focus. When you focus on the lives of others, such competitive nature transfers over to your personal loving relationships, which is often the key place where one searches for love. In your spouse is where you often seek love, validation, and affirmation. I would strongly encourage you to find everything you need from a mate in yourself and through your relationship with God first, as this is true wholeness—and wholeness leads to successful, long-lasting relationships. It is not your spouse's responsibility to make up for the areas in which you feel insecure or inferior. You must take responsibility for your own wellness by addressing areas of insecurity. Insecurity, an inward feeling of discomfort, positively used can prompt you to improve in the area in which you are performing below your standards.

How can you expect someone else to do something for you that you neglect to do for yourself? How can you expect another to esteem and love you when you do not see the value in yourself? People see outwardly how you see yourself inwardly. Though you may cover up your inferior feelings, someone with discernment and intuition can pick out your areas of insecurity a mile away. Many will attempt to build you up in the areas in which they can, obviously sensing that you are weak, but there are also those who will play on your perceived weakness and inferiority and use your inner frailties against you. Because of this, it would behoove you to address such inward matters before seeking affirmation, acceptance, and love from others.

In another scenario, others may think you have a weakness. Maybe you have characteristics that are not socially acceptable, but if you see those characteristics as a strength, you weaken the hand that the enemy has to play in making you feel less than because of them. In addition, seeing these alleged weaknesses as a strength will lead you out of unfruitful relationships and into first learning how to love yourself, which will set the standard and expectation for those around you. This will affect every area of your life. When you confidently know your worth, people in business have to respect you and pay full price for your service. God-ordained relationships must honor you or else risk losing you; family will have to monitor how they treat you; children will have to obey you; your job will pay you what you are worth; and colleagues will have to respect your worth or suffer the consequences—all because you have set the standard. And when you have done the inner work to overcome your inner weaknesses, you make the outer world around you line up with the sacrifice you have made inwardly.

The truth is that no one can give you your worth, your value, a positive perspective on yourself, confidence, or self-esteem, so though you may look for those qualities in a mate, you'll never find them in or through another person, because those things, dearly beloved, which God has placed within you, must come from you!

The opposite of focusing on yourself to perfect your overall quality of life is to attempt to pull others down to your level of perceived self-worth because of your incomplete inner work. This looks like being competitive with those who you feel are better qualified for a role or promotion that you desire, backbiting, gossiping, and attempting to disqualify others, thinking that this will increase your chances of promotion. Even worse, some people will engage in attempting to pull others down just for the joy of it, not even desiring to be promoted from the destitute circumstances (both inner and outer) the enemy is holding them in. These people allow the enemy to use them for no other motive or purpose than to prevent someone else from getting ahead, though they have no intention of getting ahead themselves. This amounts to free use by the enemy without a motive or a cause. Such misplaced focus can cause others to compete in their families, associations, and relationships, comparing their marital, educational, and homeownership status and overall success with that of others. Sadly, these limited-minded individuals assume that because they are excelling compared to others in their family or the world at large, they are doing well, but really they are still in the bracket of mediocre.

This same behavior can be displayed in friendship circles and more importantly in love relationships. In love relationships, if one person is not secure in who they are, they may find themselves competing with the one whom God created for them and sent to help them, not realizing that when a couple wins as a team, both partners win. When your spouse wins, you become "more than a conqueror" because you receive the benefits and spoils without having to do the work, as we are all in Christ (Romans 8:37)! No one else but you is called to your mate because you are like no one else, and you are called to the great successes and the life that God has ordained specifically for you. You really should hear me on this one. Here you come to finally realize that *there is absolutely no competition*! Therefore, you need not worry another night if you will find the right person for you, because the truth of the matter is that the right person will not be able to rest until they find you. You bring something very valuable into the life of that special person. Without you, they recognize that something great is missing. You bring something that God intentionally did not create anyone else to have or bring into the life of your intended mate. He tailor-made you specifically for your partner. You are that special missing part of them, beloved! There is no competition. This is why it's so important to see yourself the way that Christ does.

You must know that God is responsible for your love life. How do I know? Because his Word states that it is not good for man to be alone. For the very first person he created, he also created a spouse (Genesis 2:18). He then commanded them to be fruitful and to multiply. This commandment is fulfilled much easier by two people (Genesis 1:28). He paired the animals together. How much more are you to him than they (Matthew 6:26–33)? In addition, God himself is love. He so loved the world that he gave his only begotten Son that whoever shall call on him shall have everlasting life.

Given that God is responsible for your love life, you know that he is responsible for creating the mate whom he predestined for you. God has created your mate as he has created all things perfectly. Knowing that God is responsible for your love life should give you the rest and assurance you need to prepare yourself for your mate's coming by becoming your very best self as you "seek ye first the kingdom of God, and his righteousness; and all these things shall be added unto you" (Matthew 6:33).

It is very important that we spend time getting to know God and what he thinks about us before we search for a mate and hope that he or she will answer those questions. God not only perfects you and prepares you for your calling but also prepares you for the mate that he has for you! Seeing that he created your intended mate, who better to go to than God, to allow him to perfect you for the person he has created for you? Statistics say that there are more men in the world than women, and if your faith is in statistics, then you will have what the statistics say you will have. But "if ye have faith as a grain of mustard seed," it matters not how old you are, what your waist size is, how much money you have in your bank account, or the educational level you have reached; you shall have whatever you believe (Matthew 17:20). You must understand that when God created your mate, he was well aware of the chances that your mate would locate the wrong woman or man. He was also aware of how many women and men would be in the world during the time when your mate was attempting to find you. He has numbered our hairs; surely he has numbered the members in his universe (Luke 12:7). The solution to this is simple: rest in knowing that God created your mate just like he has provided you with food, clothes, shoes, work, shelter, transportation, and every other thing you need for your life. God is equally responsible for your love life so that you may fulfill his commandment to be fruitful and multiply.

> The more you compete by operating in someone else's lane, trying to be like your sister for example, the more self-hate and low self-esteem resides in you and the more your focus is off yourself and on the life and works of another. Then your intended mate will be unable to find the authentic version of the man or woman that he or she was uniquely designed and created to look for.

Most people who marry for destiny often say of their mate, "It was like we knew each other before meeting." That's because God built your mate to like your perfume, your body size, your career field, the way you laugh, how many children you have, where you work, the way you think, how you get along with your family, your perception, the way you walk, and the way you rub his hands. He is built innately to like everything about *you*! So it doesn't matter that there are a million other women, or that his mother doesn't like you, or that his baby mama has found fault in you, or that their children aren't interested in accepting you. The truth is that God designed him to like and love most everything about you. However, without you perfecting yourself and becoming the best version of yourself, your mate may not be able to find you. Or once he does, he may be unfulfilled and in search of a better version of you, that is, who God created you to be. For this cause, you no longer have to compete or compromise your body in trying to get him to like you, because he was created to love you.

The question is, to what degree do you love, embrace, and value yourself? I ask because as you feed yourself positivity, as you soak in God's love for you, and as you make yourself a focused priority in your life, you, much like a plant that is watered, will begin to grow and flourish, becoming all that God created you to be, exploring all that he placed within you and thereby becoming everything your mate ever wanted and envisioned. You see, God is fair. He wouldn't send you someone for whom you must compete or create someone for you and then make him more attracted to or compatible with another person. When such a thing occurs, it is the trick and work of the enemy. Know that anything sent from Satan can be countered by faith in God. This is true especially if you have experienced infidelity in your marriage.

Feeling like you are not enough is a lie from the devil. God's Word is true: "Perfect love cast out fear and the lies that create that fear" (1 John 4:18). So, no, you don't have to be intimidated by your sister's singing gift or your brother's natural gift for teaching. You don't have to bring that into your spousal relationship with the subconscious thought that you are not enough. You don't have to carry self-doubt into your parenting by comparing your child's success to another's, and you don't have to compete with your spouse's ex.

> Beloved, if no one ever told you,
> trust me: you are enough!

If you don't feel you are enough, it's simply because you are in the wrong environment, because the environment that God created for you is one he created you to fit into perfectly! He would never create a human being and place her in water, because she is not a fish. If you are not loved and accepted in your current environment, then more than likely where you are is a temporary location and you are just passing through. When it comes to what thoughts you are thinking about yourself, if you are feeding yourself "less than" thoughts of competition, comparing yourself to your partner's ex or pondering how much money her ex-husband made, then these thoughts telling you that you are not enough could be what is manifesting in your environment. What the Bible says is true: "As a man thinketh in his heart, so is he" (Proverbs 23:7). Your imagination should be used to see yourself thriving, going higher, and excelling. It is your responsibility to constantly be "casting down imaginations, and every high thing that exalteth itself against the knowledge of God, and bringing into captivity every thought to the obedience of Christ" (2 Corinthians 10:5).

If you're competing, could it be not because you're not wonderful but because others are not seeing or receiving you right? Maybe you shouldn't lower your standards and feel less than you are worth by remaining in a place of compromise. Maybe you shouldn't get the reconstructive surgery to look more socially acceptable. Maybe you shouldn't feel forced to lose weight immediately after giving birth. Maybe you shouldn't feel pressured to make or give money you currently don't have. Maybe you don't have to place your kids in private school to keep up with your in-laws. Instead of comparing yourself and using the measuring stick of others, have you ever considered just walking away? Understand this: the day you begin to compromise yourself, allowing someone to devalue and mistreat you, is the day you begin to lose the very relationship you are attempting to maintain.

> When you lose yourself, you have practically lost it all.

The more you hold fast to who you are, the more you force your potential spouse, friend, or employer to see your worth. Then they will either rise to the occasion and pay the full price of your worth to walk and remain with you or decide that price is too high. Let them go if they so choose. You owe it to them to find what makes them happy. I can assure you, beyond any shadow of a doubt, their walking away is a sign that God himself has upgraded you, so definitely wait on what is coming next, which will be better.

Wait for the one who has more in every area of life to offer you as you walk together in agreement. And more than anything, wait for the one who can offer you more *love.* You must love yourself enough to leave the presence of those who do not value you if you have learned to accept environments of rejection, as previously discussed. Know that in walking away, which sometimes you must do, you reestablish your standards and teach others how to love you as they must learn to love you the way you deserve to be loved. Maybe if you get off the path of trying to keep up with the Joneses, a trail that's not designed for you and not purposed by God, it will prevent you from missing your divine appointment with destiny and the purposed mate God has for you. If you perfect the person God has created you to be, and if your intended mate simultaneously perfects who they were created to be, which is someone whom God has made you innately to solely fit with, it will cause you to meet your God-given mate and allow your relationship with this person to soar in the process. This is what your daddy never told you and your mother never knew about real love.

It would be difficult to discuss such relationship topics and not discuss the scars of your past. By the time I was twenty-eight years old, God did a rebirth in me because I had encountered so many of life's letdowns—including much physical abuse from caregivers when I was a child and the resulting emotional rejection—that the relationships I was attracted to as an adult were toxic. During this period of rebirth, I wondered how people could survive to see age fifty-five without undergoing a rebirthing process or else having a mental breakdown, as it was super clear to me that I was doing life wrong. During this process, I spent a lot of time with God reevaluating how people had treated me but, even more so, looking at what was in me that allowed such mistreatment from others. My best friend whom I talked to every day was extremely negative. She daily talked about the good parts of my relationship in a bad way. Every positive thing I attempted to do to advance myself, she rose against it as though she were the judge and jury in our conversations. My questions to myself were, why did I regularly allow such negative friendships and relationships in my life? Why did I answer the phone when such people called? Why did I lend an ear to someone who consistently spoke negatively about the better parts of me? I encountered infidelity in my love relationships. The truth is that I had accumulated a few relationships that were the same. I began to wonder why I didn't demand a devoted commitment.

The Lord revealed to me, "Romonica, you attract who you are, and idolatry in men looks different from idolatry in women." The Lord showed me how I had placed men before him. There were times I would skip church to stay home or times when I would knowingly disobey God's Word that it was better to marry than to burn (1 Corinthians 7:8–9). I put my devotion to men above God's Word. I had made God feel the same way that I was made to feel in my cheating relationships. My goodness. I decided to make an everlasting change! It was clear that much of what I was suffering was stuff I had brought on myself. I was attracted to unhealthy, jealousy-based friendships because those people were only saying aloud what I felt within myself. And I had only felt that way about myself because I grew up in a household with people who told me what I couldn't be and that was filled with verbal, physical, and emotional abuse toward me. I was the girl whose single mother couldn't raise her because of a mental breakdown. Talk about faith. But, oh, how people judge your outcome based on your circumstances. I took ownership of my thoughts about myself and changed my own mind.

Despite your situation now, you must know that faith is the equalizer. If you have faith, you can become something different from what others in your circumstances become. If you trust that God makes no mistakes and that everything you had or did not have is going to work for your good, then you will have what you believe (Mark 9:23). You will certainly survive. And not only will you survive, beloved, but also you'll thrive with a testimony and life experiences that will only give God glory! The rebirth process I underwent with God allowed me to remain in his presence a substantial amount of time to offset the toxic childhood environments in which I grew up and had replicated in my adult life. My reading God's Word and spending quality time with him gave God time to redefine how I saw myself through his eyes and to positively replace those negative thoughts I had about myself with positive thoughts. I knew I was loved, called, and favored by him, and this outweighed the rejection I experienced from both parents, whatever society said was acceptable, every negative word spoken and received, and every toxic relationship and friendship. I didn't see myself as a burden anymore, but I came to know that I was a major asset. After this rebirth process, I sought and obtained better relationships and heightened my standards, and even in my career I began to charge what my wealth of knowledge was fully worth. I began to win in every area of my life personally and professionally. Whomever couldn't afford to pay with respect to the value that God had placed inside me was escorted out of my life. Considering his Son paid the highest price to die for me, I wasn't going to allow anything to cheapen me or bring me down from the place where God himself had set me (Ephesians 2:6). But I wasn't able to accomplish this until the Lord redefined me and revolutionized how I saw myself and thought about myself from the inside out.

I asked God why he had allowed me to grow up in a house with a mother who was schizophrenic. He responded, "Romonica, I am God. I could have allowed you to lose your mind, then turned around to give it back to you, and then called you to become a counselor and serve others through your personal experience. But I allowed the closest person to you, being your mother, to experience the mental breakdown so that you could be close enough to witness it, observe the symptoms, and see how to treat them. Then you could share your story with others without having to experience the actual breakdown yourself." My word, to think of the goodness of our God! When I shared this revelation with my mother, she cried tears. My mother does not cry easily, but her hardship and her entire life began to make sense to her that very moment when she came to know that her mental breakdown experience could be used for the purpose of God, not only so that she may know him as a healer but also so that it would have a positive influence on her daughter's career—and now on you too! Had my mother not experienced such hardship, I would have never found my God-given destiny.

What are you pregnant with that will in time come back and deliver you, beloved? I have come to know that the cost of greatness is often generational. You may be called to be the deliverer of your family or of your international community. You may never have learned the formula of deliverance had someone close to you, perhaps in your family—or even you yourself—not been bound. Allow God to turn your generational curses into generational blessings. I am a witness that he can!

chapter 21

What Are You Using?

God asked Moses, "Moses, what's in your hand?" After you have done all that you know to do and you feel as though there are no more spiritual warfare tools available for you, that you have hit the limit, adhere to this: "Having done all, to stand. Stand therefore, having your loins girt about with truth, and having on the breastplate of righteousness"

(Ephesians 6:13–14).

I will tell you to stand after you have been faithful to weekly Bible study and Sunday service church, after you have committed to reading the Word of God daily, after you have acquired a fervent prayer life, after you have committed to fasting weekly, after you have purchased relevant books and study tools on warfare that you utilize routinely, after you have cut off negative associations and sources, after you are in daily worship with the

Lord, after you seek God in daily conversation to obtain minute-by-minute instructions, after you have learned to seek deliverance from any known sin that may have you spiritually bound, after your lamenting and repenting before the Lord, after seeking deliverance from anything that may be counterproductive to your breakthrough, and after you have lain prostrate before God to express your total dependency on him. Stand! After you have "humble[d] yourselves therefore under the mighty hand of God, that he may exalt you in due time," after you have listened to sermon messages from trusted sources led by the Holy Spirit, after you have attended God-led conferences and prayer watches, after you have sought the Lord without ceasing, after you have pled the pure blood of Jesus, after you have forgiven so as not to be held back from your breakthrough, after you have asked God, "Create in me a clean heart, O God; and renew a right spirit within me," stand! Having practiced casting down every imagination, pled the blood of Jesus on every generational curse, and stood on the Word of God with your faith, praying always without ceasing, stand (1 Thessalonians 5:17)! I will also add to your standing stance the question, "Look around; what is in your hand?"

First look at your name. What does your name stand for, beloved? My mother was paranoid schizophrenic, and she named me Romonica. Unbeknown to her, the name Monica means counselor. She birthed what she needed. I became a counselor and have opened up two counseling agencies under the name of Eclectic Counseling Services, one in New Orleans and another Baton Rouge, Louisiana. Abram, who had no children for many of his married years, found the name Abraham when God changed his name, which means "father of many." Sarai's name was changed to Sarah. Jacob, a trickster with a cunning nature, found purpose in his name when God changed it to Israel, meaning "prince," standing for royalty but also indicating a prince over ruling principalities (Genesis 17:5, 15). By taking on a righteous nature and allowing God to establish the promise in him, Jacob became a force to be reckoned with who was able to withstand both spiritual forces and the forces of humankind (Genesis 32:28). The question is, what promise did God speak into existence when he called you by name? The meaning of your name can be a hint to your purpose, your promise, and your destiny and can sustain you during times of opposition. Once you come into the knowledge of the meaning of your name, if it is favorable to your circumstances, stand in that place and do not let God go until he blesses you (Genesis 32:26). In the Bible, people often named a place according to what had occurred in that particular location. "And Jacob called the name of the place Peniel; for I have seen God face to face, and my life is preserved" (Genesis 32:30). If a named place can have meaning to it, certainly a named person can produce purpose.

The next thing I would urge you to look at is your birth date. It's true that numbers matter. What day were you born? David was the eighth child. Eight means new beginnings. Where he was in the birth order was an indication that God was no longer choosing a king who had the heart of the people but was choosing a new king who had a heart after God. People look at the outer person, but God looks at the heart (1 Samuel 16:7). When facing a stubborn battle, David found that his birth order stopped his blessing from going to one of his better-thought-of siblings. God's decision to do a new thing blocked the hand of the enemy from stealing David's destined crown as king. There may come a time when the enemy will attempt to use everything known to humankind to block you from reaching your promise. And after you have done all to stand, having used every spiritual weapon the Holy Spirit has advised, you must understand, "For we wrestle not against flesh and blood, but against principalities, against powers, against the rulers of the darkness of this world, against spiritual wickedness in high places" (Ephesians 6:12), after which point, you should review your birth order or, better yet, your birth date. What was heaven numerically declaring the day that you came to earth? What is your tool of warfare for your final round that this time the Lord has strategically placed directly in your hand?

The day you were born is often heaven's declaration to the earth that is specifically in alignment with what God desires to bring forth in and through your life. The day you were born will often explain the nature of your warfare as often the enemy will assign others to abort your divinely given earthly assignment. Yet this is often the hint that you *must*, having done all, stand on this assignment. What you stand on and meditate on will produce results.

There was a time in my life when I had tried everything I knew to do, yet the enemy kept coming against my God-given assignment. He was persistent. My date of birth is August 17. Eight means a new beginning, and seventeen means victory. My date of birth spoke to me, saying that the new beginning shall have victory. I was called to break several generational curses on my family, but when the cycle hit my life personally, I, having done all to stand, stood on heaven's assignment, hidden and tucked into the right pocket of my date of birth. This spoke and proved true that the new beginning would have victory and break the cycle of misfortune. I placed my weight on my faith in God and the new beginning that God himself would establish in me. I stood on that new beginning and did not move until it was not only manifested but also established. This uprooted failure produced *victory* in the area that I was trusting in God for. I have tried this for myself. Beloved, what is your name? Moreover, what does your heaven-given date of birth speak to you? Look around; what is in your hand?

chapter 22

The Spirit of Rejection

There may come a point when the thing that is attempting to overtake you begins to manifest in the works or actions of either yourself, through self-sabotaging behaviors, or others known as promise enemies. When the children of Israel set out to obtain their freedom, before they ever made it to their Promised Land, a pharaoh spirit attempted to keep them in bondage, to hold them hostage, as if there was an earthly figure that would not allow them to go free. This was beyond the limitations of being just spiritual. There will come a time when, if there is something attempting to keep you from the set promise of God, you will have to ask God to reveal to you the spiritual nature and origin of this matter. There may be someone attempting to stop you from being promoted to that manager position. Your babysitter may be stopping you from taking night college courses. Demonic forces may have been coming against you in your season for promotion, ministry, healing, finances, marriage, increase, and the promises of God. Your job is to place focus not on the person but on the door through which the spirit of the manifestation entered. In short, how is it that

God is allowing this to happen? Just as there are natural laws commanding us not to steal, shoplift, kill, or engage in domestic violence, so there are also spiritual laws.

What in your life has granted legal access to that which is attacking your promise? For the children of Israel, it is clear that many of them had a spirit of unbelief to the point that they murmured against God, thinking that they would never reach their place of promise and desiring to return to bondage by becoming Pharaoh's slaves again (Exodus 16:3). Never mind that Pharaoh had drowned in the Red Sea and the children of Israel could not return to him per se (Exodus 15:4). The children of Israel suffered with a spirit of disbelief after being set free. It could have been that same spirit of disbelief that gave access to Pharaoh and that had manifested physically to hinder them from breaking free to begin with.

What unbelief there is in you has manifested the very thing that is now coming against your breakthrough, promise, overflow, victory, and abundance. This disbelief will cause you to compromise and thereby abort the promise that God intends to make come true for you. Many who have difficulty locating true, sincere love are oftentimes those who have experienced failed love or who have a history of rejection. Love, in essence, is favor. When the king chose Esther, he first favored her, meaning that she was chosen as his favorite (Esther 2:1). Being favored equates to being chosen and loved above any other. Joseph's father loved, favored, and esteemed Joseph above Joseph's brothers. The opposite of being loved is to be hated. To be hated is to be rejected, unchosen, or looked over. Leah was hated by Jacob because he favored her sister over her and therefore chose someone else instead of her. Jesus was rejected by human beings, but he did not carry a spirit of rejection. Jesus understood that being rejected by humankind was bearable because he knew the true love of his Father God.

When you take on a spirit of rejection, it may be because you weren't your mother's favorite. Maybe you've experienced divorce. Maybe your earthly biological father didn't claim you as his own. To take on a spirit of rejection is to allow the rejected event to take root in your spirit, where you feel like there is something wrong with you or that you're unlovable because you were rejected by another. Sometimes rejection is simply an indication of redirection, transition, temporal circumstance, or protection; it's not always to be taken personally. If you wish ever to find love or to attract favor again into your life, you must denounce that spirit of rejection and understand that rejection is not a reflection of who you are. That you were rejected by a particular person was the will of God because he felt you were deserving of so much better. Keep in mind that Jesus died so that you may live abundantly, so that you may have the true desires of your heart, which is God's expected end for your life. For this reason you must trust the Creator of heaven and earth. Surely he is qualified to handle your affairs (John 10:10). In addition, you must understand that your experience of rejection neither defines you nor determines your future.

You are not who left or what happened to you. You may be unloved by one, but you are loved by so many others. In addition, you are loved by our Father God to the point that he will not allow you to settle. Nor will he allow anything to remain in your life that is not capable of building you up (John 15:2). Those who are gone from your life did not leave you; God removed them because he is protective of you. To be rejected by human beings often means you are chosen by God. He will handpick every detail of your life and remove anything that is not to his standards or to his liking concerning you. Take off that coat of bitterness, loss, low self-esteem, and depression, and put on your coat of many colors. Think on whatsoever is lovely, the positive things about yourself, and the pluses people get when they get you, including your gifts, your talents, and your strengths. Think on those things, building yourself up as worthy no matter what you don't have or who went missing (Isaiah 61:3). It's not what you don't have that you need to enter into the Promised Land. It is your confidence in the God who chose you before the foundation of the earth; stand on that thought, and make earth obey the decree and order of your God, who thought enough about you to choose you. That alone overrules the rejection of your past, your enemies, the spirit of rejection/disbelief, and any obstacle currently standing in your way.

chapter 23

You Never Have to Compete for Love

There is only one you. Who can compete with the uniqueness of all that God has placed within you? Focus on your strengths and not your weaknesses.

Understand that jealousy and envy highlight your weaknesses and also highlight the strengths of the person of whom you are jealous.

It would benefit us to place all our focus on God's plans for our lives, become who he created us to be, and ensure that we keep our hearts pure in relation to how we see ourselves and others. After all, the way to have an overall healed, healthy, whole, and victorious life is to guard your heart with diligence, for out of it flows the issues of life (Proverbs 4:13). This means that if you place your focus and attention on competing, comparing, or bringing others down, you will apprehend your own life as you bitterly watch your alleged opponents excel. Even if the opponent is your ex who wronged and betrayed you, God will avenge you (Romans 12:19). However, if you place your focus on the things that we have discussed, such as your healing, forgiving, and self-love, it will propel you, excel you, and refocus your life toward total victory (Proverbs 4:23)!

chapter 24

Your Graduation

Scars are your badge of honor and life's
tools to aid you to reach higher ground.

How are you looking at your scars? Avoid looking at them through the lens of bitterness.

Let's talk about your past scars and pains. First you must understand that your scars are an indication of the area in which God desires to promote you. Your scars are a collection of lessons that you've learned in a particular area based on your prior experiences. I have never attended a class where I didn't learn a set of lessons from the chapters of the textbook and which I didn't eventually pass, only to graduate to the next level after a given period of time. Consider middle school for instance. You didn't take six different courses with their series of quizzes, tests, midterms, projects, bonus assignments, attendance requirements, and exit exams only to remain at the same grade level and repeat the same courses the year after, did you?

As it is in school, so it is in life. Your scars are proof that you not only took a test or a life exam but also learned the lessons from it. Some blessings only come after you have taken the necessary prerequisites or learned the lessons to prepare for them. Many people want to be promoted but do not have the experience or understanding to maintain the position if God were to grant it to them. This is because they have not learned the lessons and therefore have no scars in the area in which they hope to be promoted. Scars are proof that you qualify for the breakthrough.

There are some promotions that God desires to give you, but the lessons that you need to learn were not taught in a classroom or during conversations with your friends. Your church might have given you general but not directly specific information uniquely pertaining to the sensitivity of your situation. And if you are breaking a generational curse, there is no family member to show you the ropes of promotion in this particular matter. If the foregoing circumstances apply to you, then you, beloved, qualify for the test of scars, meaning that life is possibly getting ready to qualify you for your next blessing. But it may come about in what older people call "the hard way," by way of scars. Having scars means you learned the lessons the hard way, which has qualified you for a greater breakthrough!

The next step is understanding why you have to qualify for a promotion. If God chose you, why can't you just receive the blessing without the hard lessons? Some substantial blessings require a foundation, and that foundation is a collection of characteristics that are necessary for you to not only secure the blessing but also maintain your promotion. When you are looking for a job, most prospective employers ask for a résumé to determine if you have the work experience necessary to qualify for the position you are applying for. Some jobs ask that you meet certain criteria, and if you do not meet those criteria, they determine that the position is beyond your ability. Your scars are proof that you have the humility, work ethic, character, stamina, emotional wellness, resilience, and so forth that your promotion requires and that justify you for the promotion. Since God does not specialize in failure, he is sure to prep you for all the difficulties that will come along with your promotion prior to your receiving the advancement so as to prevent you from being demoted for being ill-equipped. Your scars are proof that you have learned the hard way to put God first and honor his will and Word in the area that you expect him to promote you in.

Promotion comes from God, beloved (Psalm 75:6–7). If you are waiting on marriage, you should have learned through your scars to remain abstinent until marriage. If you are believing for a financial increase because you are currently experiencing financial hardship, the lesson you may have learned through your scars is to pay your tithes, honoring and trusting God above all else in your finances. The lesson is to strengthen you in the very area that you were weak in that caused you to lose the original battle. Scars are the only proof that you have improved in the area in which you previously failed.

Without learning and being strengthened in the area you were once weak in, which weakness caused you to lose the battle before, what guarantees do you have that you will not make the same mistake and fail the same test the very same way again if the opportunity to be tested again presents itself? Your scars tell God, "I have learned and therefore have intelligence, discipline, and strength and have received correction in the area in which I once was lacking. Therefore, you can trust me to retake this test of promotion and to pass it, dear God."

> Becoming bitter keeps you stuck and stagnant as bitterness keeps you focused on what has been lost as opposed to being focused on the necessary preparation for the test retake.

Your preparation will require you to process your last loss. You will have to consider what failed tools you brought to the test from your bloodline that might have presented as a generational curse, therefore leading to a repeating generational cycle of failure in that particular area. What did you take into that test as "truth" that opposed what the Word of God has spoken about you, as you are the head and not the tail, above only and not beneath (Deuteronomy 28:13)? After examining and processing the cause of your scars with the Holy Spirit, you, like any champion preparing for battle, will have to meditate and purposely correct those things before your retake, if one is required. You must correct these failures prior to the arrival of your promise. To correct them in the midst of your retake is to once again arrive at the door of opportunity unprepared! Prepare now for your promotion. Scars are nothing more than proof that you have taken the necessary classes and learned the lessons required for your nearing graduation. Blessings.

What your daddy never told you and your mother never knew is that both life and love may require high-level warfare. But fight anyway.

Printed in the United States
By Bookmasters